BREAKFAST WITH BILLY GRAHAM

BREAKFAST WITH BILLY GRAHAM

120 DAILY READINGS

Compiled and edited by

Bill Deckard

TESTAMENT BOOKS
NEW YORK

This 2003 edition is published by Testament Books, an imprint of Random House Value Publishing, a division of Random House, Inc., New York, by arrangement with Servant Publications.

Random House
New York • Toronto • London • Sydney • Auckland
www.randomhouse.com

Interior photos: Bettmann, New York, NY. Used by permission.

Printed and bound in Singapore.

A catalog record for this title is available from the Library of Congress.

ISBN 0-517-22255-8

10 9 8 7 6 5 4 3 2 1

*B*ecause of God's love there is a way of salvation, a way back to God through Jesus Christ, his Son.

But God will not force himself upon us against our will. If we want his love, we need to believe in him. We need to make a definite, positive act of commitment and surrender to the love of God. No one can do it for us. We can hear all the days of our lives about the love of God and yet die without Christ. Or we can open our hearts today and say, "Yes, my heart is open; I receive Christ."

"Lord, Please Change Me."

The Bible says that God is love (1 John 4:8). He loves you. He is interested in you. He has the hairs of your head numbered (Matthew 10:30). He loves you with an everlasting love (Jeremiah 31:3). And he wants to forgive you. He wants to come into your life and into your home and into your work and into all relationships and help you….

I remember the night that I committed my life to Christ. It was at an evangelistic meeting. I went forward, because I deeply wanted Christ. I knew that I really didn't know Christ, that I didn't have a personal relationship with him.

That night I got on my knees beside my bed and I said, "Oh, God, I don't know much about what I've done tonight, and I certainly don't know much about You. But what little I do know, please change me and make me a new person."

From that night on I was different. God had taken over my life and began to move in my life in the most marvelous way.

2
The Lonely Rebel

In John 13 we read the story of the Last Supper and the prophecies about the betrayal by Judas. Judas went out, Scripture says, and "it was night" (John 13:30). He betrayed the Lord. He had no fellowship with Christ from that moment on.

Perhaps there was a time when you knew the fellowship of God. You walked with him. You attended church. You read the Bible. You were faithful in the way you lived. But now gradually you have changed, and you don't walk as closely with the Lord as you once did. There was a time when you had peace with God. But you went out from his presence, and you found that it was night; the night of loneliness for God settled over you.

But you can come back. You can make it right. God stands with open arms and says, "Come back. I love you. I will forgive you. I will receive you." Perhaps there is no loneliness quite so bitter as the loneliness of a person who attends church but doesn't know Christ personally. Many people are like that. Sin makes us lonely because it separates us from God.

3
We Must Be Born Again

We cannot be born a Christian. We have to be born again (John 3:5, 7). "Born from above" is what that really means. Jesus said, "Except ye be converted, and become as little children, you shall not enter into the kingdom of heaven" (Matthew 18:3). Jesus said that to enter the Kingdom of Heaven, we have to be converted.

Have you been converted? To be converted means to be changed, to let Christ come into your heart and satisfy that longing you have. Many of you have an empty place in your life, and you don't know what is causing it. You have troubles in your family. You have troubles in your community. You have troubles at work. And you don't know how to get out of these troubles. You are caught in some sort of a trap. Maybe it is a drug habit that you can't throw off, or maybe it is some other habit. Would you like to be free? You need Christ, and he can help you.

Jesus said, "Ye shall know the truth, and the truth shall make you free" (John 8:32). Jesus Christ can come into your heart and forgive your sins, cleanse you and change you. Christ stands ready to give hope to everyone. Christ's truth can make you free.

4
Three Steps to Salvation

You ask, "What do I have to do to find salvation?" First, you must repent of your sins.... The word "repent" means to change—change your mind, change your lifestyle. You are going in one direction; you turn and go in another.

But you cannot repent by yourself. God has to help you to repent. And he will help, but you need to be willing. You need to say, "Lord, I want to repent, but You will have to help me to change."

Second, you must believe. "Believe" means that you rest totally upon God and God alone. You are not trusting your family to save you; you are not trusting your husband or your wife to save you; you are not trusting the Church to save you. You are trusting Christ, and Christ alone....

The Bible says, "As many as received him, to them gave he power to become the sons of God, even to them that believe on his name" (John 1:12). You need to put your total weight on Christ.

Then you must confess Christ openly: "If thou shalt confess with thy mouth the Lord Jesus, and shalt believe in thine heart that God hath raised him from the dead, thou shalt be saved" (Romans 10:9).

That is how you come to Christ. You must repent. You must believe. You must confess.

5

The Scholars Heard a Simple Sermon

One time I was preaching in Africa to a small group of tribal people. I was told that this tribe had not heard much about the Gospel, and I wanted to bring a simple Gospel message. So I preached on John 3:16 as simply as I knew how. Trying to explain John 3:16, I used every illustration I could think of that would make the message clear. Several people indicated that they wanted to receive Christ.

The next Sunday I was to preach at the parish church of Great St. Mary at Cambridge University in England, and I thought, "I'm going to try something. I am going to preach the same simple sermon at Cambridge that I preached to the tribe in Africa." And I did. It was a simple exposition on John 3:16. That Sunday many of those students came to know Christ as Lord and Savior.

6
She Was Won to Christ by His Tears

One of our associate evangelists was preaching at a university. He tried to win the students to Christ, but their reaction was hostile. One young woman was especially hostile. After the lecture she came to him and said, "I don't believe anything you said."

He said, "I'm sorry that you don't agree, but do you mind if I pray for you?"

She answered, "Nobody ever prayed for me before; I guess it won't do any harm."

He bowed his head and began to pray. She stood looking straight ahead. But suddenly she noticed that while he was praying, tears were coming down his cheeks. When he opened his eyes, she was in tears. She said, "No one in my entire life has shed a tear for me." They sat on a bench and that woman accepted Christ as her Savior.

How many of us have loved others so much that we have shed tears for them?

7
Messages of Hope in the Night

It is significant that the angel's message to the shepherds was delivered at night. It was night not only because the sun had gone down, but because the world was enshrouded in spiritual and moral gloom. It is often when things are darkest that God manifests himself.

It was night in Egypt when the children of Israel were released from the bondage of Pharaoh. It was night when Samuel discerned the voice of God calling him to be a prophet to God's people. It was at night that God gave David some of his sweetest psalms. It was night when Paul and Silas prayed and sang praises in the Philippian jail. And it was night when Christ was born in Bethlehem, when the angel of the Lord made the glorious proclamation that a Savior had been given.

To many of you now it is night too. It is night in your hospital room; it is night because of distress and bereavement. But I want to tell you that above the clouds, the sun is shining. You can receive Christ into your heart, and he can bring joy, and a thrill, and glory such as you have never known—if you will give your life to him.

8
The Wonder of God's Love

Consider the wonder of God's love. Almighty God, the Creator of the whole universe, loves you and is interested in you, as if you were the only person who ever lived. He loves you so much that he gave his only Son for you (see John 3:16).

Loneliness is one of the greatest problems people face. We can be in a crowd, we can be at a party, and we can all of a sudden feel lonely. Do you know what that is? That is loneliness for God. We were made in the image of God, made for fellowship with God. That fellowship has been broken by sin, and so we are lonely for God. We don't find fulfillment or purpose or meaning in life because we are without God. That is why Christ came. He came to bring us to God....

Jesus Christ loved us from the cross where he shed his blood for us. That is the only cleansing power that will wash away sin—the blood of Christ which was shed on the cross for you. If you turn away from his love, there is no hope.

When we have disobeyed God, he still wants to put his arms around us and say, "I love you." From the cross God is saying to us, "I love you."

At age 36, Billy Graham had been heard by millions. He was predicted to become the greatest evangelist of our time.

9

The Wonder of the Incarnation

Consider also the wonder of God's coming to live among us: "The Word was made flesh, and dwelt among us" (John 1:14). That is a tremendous thing. It means that the whole of everything that we can think of came to dwell among us. God became a man. He became flesh so that he might experience our temptations…. He understands us.

One time when I was speaking at Harvard University, a young German student told me the story of a little girl in Germany who came home from Sunday school and asked, "Mommy, where is God?"

"Oh, darling," replied her mother, "God is everywhere."

The little girl said, "But I don't want God to be everywhere. I want God to be somewhere, and I want him to be somebody."

God is in Christ…. The incarnation of Christ is not merely a doctrinal tenet. It is a glorious reality, a wondrous fact, apart from which there could be no salvation for sinful people.

10
The Wonder of the Cross

There is also the wonder of the cross. "My God, my God, why hast thou forsaken me?" (Matthew 27:46) is the cry from the cross. What happened in that moment? …

Jesus Christ was dying for you and for me. But he wasn't just dying the physical death from the nails in his hands and the spear in his side and the crown of thorns on his brow and the lashing of his back with a leather whip with steel pellets on the end. That was his physical suffering. But his spiritual suffering came when God laid on him your sins and my sins. Scripture says he became sin for us (see 2 Corinthians 5:21). He became guilty of adultery, murder, lust, greed, pride, and everything that you can think of. He had never known sin, but he took the penalty for all our sin.…

He took the judgment and the hell that we deserve. The Bible says, "The wages of sin is death" (Romans 6:23). That means judgment and hell. I deserve judgment. I am a sinner. I have broken God's Law. I deserve the judgment that is coming to me. But instead of that judgment striking me, it struck Christ. That is what the cross is all about. That is why the cross is the great symbol of Christianity.…

How wonderful to know that my sins are gone. "There is therefore now no condemnation to them which are in Christ Jesus" (Romans 8:1).

11
The Wonder of Conversion

And consider the wonder of conversion. Jesus said, "Except ye be converted, and become as little children, ye shall not enter into the kingdom of heaven" (Matthew 18:3). The word "converted" confuses some people. We think we have to have great emotion. That lightning has to strike or something has to happen. Rather, we are asked to say "no" to sin and "yes" to Christ....

People come to Christ in different ways. I came to Christ very simply. I remember that I was a member of the church, vice president of the young people's society in our church, and I thought I was all right. Everybody considered me to be a good boy. But down deep in my heart I knew there was something missing. I couldn't wait to leave home so that I wouldn't have to go to church.

But one night I went to an evangelistic meeting. I went several nights, and the Spirit of God spoke to me and I gave my heart to Jesus Christ. The next day I knew something had happened. I didn't know what, but I knew I was different. I went along for about a year and I began to want to read the Bible and go to church. That simple act of saying "yes" to Christ changed my life.

12
What If Christ Had Not Come?

Have you ever thought about what has happened because Christ has come to the world? Our world has felt the mighty impact of Jesus Christ. His compassion has made the world more compassionate; his healing touch has made the world more humanitarian; his selflessness has made the world more unselfish; his sacrifice has made the world more self-effacing. Christ drew a rainbow of hope around the shoulders of men and women and gave them something to live for. If Christ had not come, this world would indeed be a hopeless world. If Christ had not come, this would be a lost world. There would be no access to God; there would be no atonement; there would be no forgiveness; there would be no Savior.

Is he your Savior? Have you invited him into your heart? Or is your life like the congested little inn in Bethlehem—too crowded for Christ? If you have everything except Christ, you still have nothing; but if you have little else besides Christ, you have everything.

13

Christmas on Heartbreak Ridge

During the Korean War, one Christmas Eve a young Marine lay dying on Heartbreak Ridge. The chaplain climbed up the slope and stooped over the Marine and whispered, "May I help you, son?"

"No, it's all right," he answered.

The chaplain marveled at the young man's complacency in such an hour; then, glancing down, the chaplain noticed a New Testament clutched in the Marine's hand. And the reason for the young man's tranquility was found on the page where his finger was inserted: "My peace I give unto you" (John 14:27).

Today, in the midst of trouble, terrorism, and war, that peace can be yours. It can come if you put your faith in Jesus Christ....

The gift of eternity can be ours now. "He who has the Son has life; he who has not the Son has not life" (1 John 5:12, RSV). This is the real meaning of Christmas.

14

He Loves You No Matter What

No matter what sin we have committed, God loves us. We may be at the gate of hell itself, but God loves us with eternal love. Because he is a holy God, our sins have separated us from him. But thanks be to God; because of his love there is a way of salvation, a way back to God through Jesus Christ, his Son.

But this love of God that is immeasurable and unending, this love of God that reaches us wherever we are, can be rejected. God will not force himself upon us against our will. We can hear about the love of God and say, "No, I will not have it," and God will let us go on without his love. But if we want his love, we need to believe in him—we need to receive the love of God. We need to make a definite, positive act of commitment and surrender to the love of God. No one can do it for us. We can hear all the days of our lives about the love of God and yet die without Christ. Or we can open our hearts today and say, "Yes, my heart is open; I receive Christ."

15
"The Buck Stops Here"

President Harry Truman used to keep a little motto on his desk that read, "The buck stops here." But most of us have a tendency not to accept responsibility; we prefer to let someone else take it....

Aaron, in the Old Testament, was that way. When Moses came down from the mountain, Aaron had built a golden calf, and people were worshiping it. Moses became angry, and he broke the Tables of the Law. But Aaron didn't want to accept any responsibility for worshiping a calf. He said in effect, "Moses, don't blame me. All I did was put the gold into the fire, and it came out a calf" (see Exodus 32:24)....

People blame society. They blame the environment.... They blame circumstances. Adam sinned in a perfect environment under perfect circumstances. We can't blame our sin on someone else. Society is made up of individuals. If we have social injustice, we are the ones who are wrong; we are part of it. Let's accept our responsibility to do something about it....

In his book, *Man's Search for Meaning: An Introduction to Logotherapy,* Viktor Frankl wrote, "Everything can be taken from a man but one thing: the last of human freedoms—to choose one's own way." God has given us the power of choice.

16
Does Repentance Require Tears?

True repentance involves three things: Our mind, our emotions, and our will. First,… it means that intellectually we say, "I'm wrong. My view of God is wrong. My view of Christ is wrong. My view of my own sin is wrong."

Second, it involves the emotions. Paul wrote, "I rejoice… that ye sorrowed to repentance" (2 Corinthians 7:9). There is a certain amount of sorrow involved in repentance that we don't see much of today. I don't mean that we need to have a great emotional experience, but I do believe we need some tears of repentance. We need to be sorry for our sins….

I am not an emotional person. I don't know why, but I don't cry easily. The evening I came to Christ, I didn't have any tears. But later that night at home, I looked out my window at the North Carolina sky and I cried over my sins. Since that evening I have known that my sins were forgiven….

Third, repentance involves the will. It means that we resolve to change our way of living. It isn't easy to say, "I know that some things are wrong in my life; I know that some things should not be there; but I will change. I am willing to let God come in and change me."

17

Jesus Is Both God and Man

Jesus is not only the Christ, he is also "God, our Lord and Savior" (see Titus 2:13). This is a staggering, almost incomprehensible truth: God himself has come down on this planet in the Person of his only Son. The incarnation and the full deity of Jesus are the cornerstones of the Christian faith. Jesus Christ was not just a great teacher or a holy religious leader. He was God himself in human flesh—fully God and fully man.

Jesus himself gave frequent witness to his uniqueness and his divine nature. To his opponents he declared, "Before Abraham was, I am" (John 8:58). They immediately recognized this as a clear claim to divinity and tried to stone him for blasphemy. On another occasion Jesus stated, "I and my Father are one," and again his enemies tried to stone him, "because that thou, being a man makest thyself God" (John 10:30, 33). Furthermore, he demonstrated the power to do things that only God can do, such as forgive sins (Mark 2:1-12). The charge brought against him at his trial was that "he made himself the Son of God" (John 19:7); and when asked if he was the son of God, he replied, "You are right in saying I am" (Luke 22:70, NIV).

18
Is There Proof That Jesus Is God?

What proof did Jesus offer that he was truly God come in human form? First, there was the proof of his perfect life (see John 8:46).... Those who schemed to bring him to trial had to obtain false witnesses to bring charges, because he was blameless....

Second, there was the evidence of his power... the power only God has. He had power over the forces of nature.... He had power over sickness and disease.... His miracles were a witness to the fact that he is Lord of all nature.

Third, there was the evidence of fulfilled prophecy.... Uncounted details of his life were foretold by the prophets, and in every instance these prophecies were fulfilled (e.g., Micah 5:2; Psalm 22; Isaiah 53)....

Fourth, there was the evidence of his resurrection from the dead.... The founders of the various non-Christian religions of the world have lived, died, and been buried.... But Christ is alive! His resurrection is a fact! His tomb is empty! (see 1 Corinthians 15)....

Fifth, there is the proof of changed lives.... Education and discipline can do no more than rub off the rough edges of human selfishness—but Christ alone, the divine Son of God, has power to change the human heart....

Yes, Jesus Christ is who he said he is: God himself in human form.

19

Jesus Was Born to Be King

Jesus Christ was born to be King. From his very birth he was recognized as King. Something about him inspired allegiance, loyalty, and homage. Wise men brought him gifts. Shepherds fell down and worshiped him. And angels, knowing more than men that he was truly King, became celestial minstrels before his manger throne. Herod, realizing that there is never room for two thrones in one kingdom, sought Jesus' life.

As Jesus came to the age of approximately 30 years and began his ministry, his claims upon people's lives were total and absolute. He allowed no divided loyalty. He demanded and received complete adoration and devotion. Mature men and women left their homes, their families, and their businesses and gave themselves in complete obedience to him. Many of them gave their lives, pouring out the last full measure of devotion....

In the New Testament the entire book of Matthew is on the Kingship of Christ. People often skip the first chapter of Matthew because it contains so many "begats." It seems uninteresting to them, and they wonder why it is there. But Matthew gives this genealogy to prove Christ's royal descent.

20
Jesus Is the King of Hearts

All through his life, Christ acted like a King. He spoke with authority. He made demands upon people's consciences. He denounced bigotry, hypocrisy and greed.... He denounced immorality, dishonesty, and lawlessness. He spoke often of his coming Kingdom, and he recruited followers. His conduct was regal. His ethics were kingly.

From the beginning the potentates of political, social, and ecclesiastical life were distrustful of him. His high ethical teachings, his irreproachable moral character, and his regal lineage constantly jeopardized the security of the thrones of hypocrites.

But Herod needlessly feared Jesus. Pilate was unnecessarily suspicious of him. Christ had not come to set up an earthly kingdom. He had come to be the King of redemption. His Kingdom was to be spiritual. He was to reign in the hearts of men and women.

21
The King of Hearts Died for His People

Christ also died like a king. By virtue of his kingly office, he was the only One in heaven qualified to redeem a lost world. Had Jesus Christ been less than he was, he could not have made atonement for our sins. Fully aware of our inability to pay the price of redemption, Jesus gave himself a ransom for us.

About 800 years before Jesus' birth the prophet Isaiah wrote, "He hath poured out his soul unto death; and he was numbered with the transgressors; and he bore the sin of many, and made intercession for the transgressors" (Isaiah 53:12). What greater service could the King possibly render his subjects than to exonerate them from all guilt and to make them joint-heirs with him in his Kingdom? The King laid down his life for his subjects and made payment for the terrible debt that we owe.

Billy Graham's family greets him on the Queen Mary upon his return from a world tour, July 1954. Clockwise from the top, Ruth Bell Graham and daughters Anne, Ruth, and Virginia.

22
Christe the Risen King Reigns Today

Many people are asking, "Where is the Kingdom of God today? If he is a King, where is his Kingdom? Is it off on some distant planet or star?"

The Bible teaches that Christ does have a Kingdom on earth. His Kingdom is in the hearts of all who trust in him. He has pronounced a special blessing on those who love him. He is the undisputed King of the souls of believers of all colors and races in the world today.

Believers are still willing to die for him. He still makes unconditional demands on our lives. He still denounces sin. His presence is still incongruous with dishonesty, greed, and selfishness. His principles are still the criteria of our ethics. His teachings are still honored and revered. His selfless love is still the wonder of the universe. He still challenges us to live nobly and godly in this world. His power is still adequate to transform and to recreate the sin-cursed soul. He is the Savior of sinners, the Author of peace, and the Hope of the world.

23
My Ticket to the King's Wedding Feast

One day Christ will be King of kings and Lord of lords. There is an hour in God's time when Christ will return to this world....

Every king has a coronation. The Bible speaks of the marriage supper of the Lamb which will be the coronation of Jesus Christ. What a sight that will be! All of us who have acknowledged him as King here will be there in that Day. My reservation is made. My seat is being saved at the marriage supper of the Lamb (see Revelation 19:9). My ticket is in my heart. It is paid for by the blood of Christ upon the cross. The only thing that it cost me was my sins. I gladly renounce them and pay allegiance to the King of kings before whom some day I shall stand to give an account of my stewardship on earth.

Yes, I give my allegiance to Christ as Savior and Lord. I will work for him, and I will give him everything that I have. I will suffer for him. And some day I will have the privilege of reigning with him in Glory.

Do you know Christ? Is he King of your heart? Does the Kingdom of Christ dwell in your heart? It can, if you will open your heart and let him in today.

24
He Never Wrote a Book or Founded a College

Jesus lived in a small country and never went beyond its borders. He was so poor he said of himself that he had nowhere to lay his head. His only pocketbook was the mouth of a fish. He rode on another man's beast. He cruised the lake in another man's boat. He was buried in another man's grave. Yet he had laid aside a royal robe to do it.

He never wrote a book. His recorded words would hardly make a pocket edition. Yet all the words that have been written about him, brought together, would fill a thousand Congressional libraries.

He never founded a college to perpetuate his doctrines. Yet his teachings have endured for 2,000 years. He never carried a sword, he never organized an army, he never built a navy, he never had an air force. Yet he founded an empire in which there are millions today who would die for him.

He never studied medicine. Yet he healed those who came to him. The world would not have him. Yet when he died, the sun veiled its face and all the heavens put on mourning.

The date on the calendar as I write is 1987. Why isn't it dated from Rome's foundation, or from the French Revolution, or from Mohammed's flight, or from Buddha's birth? Because according to accepted chronology, this Man was born 1,987 years ago.

25

The Living Dead Have Heard His Voice!

The power of Christ's resurrection saves and redeems. Jesus said, "The hour is coming, and now is, when the dead shall hear the voice of the Son of God: and they that hear shall live" (John 5:25).

I have seen hundreds, yes, thousands of men and women who are among the living dead. Life to them has become a hollow mockery and a sham; life has lost its purpose and meaning. These people are bored and fed up; they have no zest for living. I have seen them come in simple, trusting faith to the living Christ. They have put their trembling hands into the strong hands of the crucified and risen Christ. I have seen them in the glow of the living Christ step out of a casket of broken hopes and dreams to become happy, useful, integrated people, filled with purpose and power.

Jesus' words have not changed. Time has not robbed them of their power. When "the dead... hear the voice of the Son of God... they that hear shall live." The Christ who lived on this planet still lives today, raising from their lifelessness all those who believe in him.

26
Are You Lonely?

Do you feel lonely? Even in a crowd, you can feel so alone. At home, that loneliness is with you. Even if your family is there, you can feel alone. Why? Because you are lonely for God.

When we were holding a Crusade in Glasgow, Scotland, a convention dealing with various human afflictions was being held there. In an address a psychiatrist said that the most frequent human hurt today is loneliness. People have dissociated from each other. Perhaps you are suffering from loneliness right now....

What we need is reconciliation to God. People are separated from God—separated by sin. Scripture teaches that we were sinners even from our mothers' wombs: "In sin did my mother conceive me" (Psalm 51:5)....

The word "sin" means to break the Laws of God. We have broken the Ten Commandments.... We are born with the tendency to sin.

But the Cross is the answer to our loneliness for God. Christ died for our sins and shed his blood on the cross. He lives to offer us new life, a life of fellowship with himself. He wraps his arms around us and says, "I love you."

27
The Loneliness of Suffering and Sorrow

Loneliness can result from suffering. When we suffer, the world ends at the foot of our beds. I have friends who are suffering in hospitals, and I want to go to these friends and put my arms around them. The Apostle Paul wrote, "I reckon that the sufferings of this present time are not worthy to be compared with the glory which shall be revealed in us" (Romans 8:18). Christ gives us the hope that our suffering will come to an end; there will be glory at the end of the suffering....

There is the loneliness of sorrow. The older I get, the more funerals I attend as friends die. Jesus wept at the funeral of a friend. He said, "I am the resurrection, and the life: he that believeth in me, though he were dead, yet shall he live: and whosoever liveth and believeth in me shall never die" (John 11:25-26). That is the hope he gives to those who are suffering in sorrow....

Scripture says, "God shall wipe away all tears from their eyes; and there shall be no more death, neither sorrow, nor crying, neither shall there be any more pain: for the former things are passed away" (Revelation 21:4). I am looking forward to that day when we will be in the presence of Christ forever!

28

His Loneliness Heals Our Loneliness

Even though great crowds surrounded Jesus at times, he was alone. And even at the end of his life, he was alone: "All the disciples forsook him, and fled" (Matthew 26:56). The crowds who had that very week shouted, "Hosanna," now began to shout, "Crucify him, crucify him!" He was alone (Matthew 21:9; Luke 23:21).

At last he cried out from the cross, "My God, my God, why hast thou forsaken me?" (Matthew 27:46) Christ, hanging on the cross, was the loneliest person who has ever lived. Why? Because he was bearing your sins and my sins on that cross, and God cannot look upon sin. Jesus was enduring for you and for me the nightmare of our judgment. That's how much he loves us….

Through his death Christ dealt with the primary cause of human loneliness: separation from God. From the cross he reaches out to you and to me….

You never have to be lonely again. An experience with Christ can fill the void and the emptiness of your life, and give you something worth living for. Do you know Christ?

29
Integrity: The Television Was Watching!

Integrity means that a person is the same on the inside as he or she is on the outside. There is no discrepancy between what he says and what he does, between his walk and his talk. A person of integrity can be trusted, and he is the same person alone a thousand miles from home as he is in church, or in his community, or in his home....

I once met the manager of a hotel who said that a religious convention had met at his hotel and that at night, when the people returned to their rooms, they would turn on the pay television. He said that 75 percent of them turned to the R-rated pictures. What a difference there is sometimes between the way we preach and the way we live.

30
Integrity: Caught in the Act of Prayer!

As a person comes to know Christ in a real and personal way, he becomes truly an individual of vision and integrity....

A young president of an East Coast company instructed his secretary not to disturb him because he had an important appointment. The chairman of the board arrived and said, "I want to see Mr. Jones."

The secretary answered, "I'm sorry. He cannot be disturbed. He has a special appointment."

The chairman became angry and banged open the door. He saw the president of the corporation in prayer. The chairman softly closed the door and asked the secretary, "Is that usual?"

She answered, "Yes, sir, every morning."

The chairman replied, "No wonder we come to him for advice."

Christ Made Me Want to Change

Paul gloried in the cross because he knew that it gave a new dynamic to life. Once you have been to the cross, you will never be the same. Scripture says, "If any man be in Christ, he is a new creature: old things are passed away; behold, all things are become new" (2 Corinthians 5:17).

I remember when I first came to Christ. I was already a member of the church. I had already been baptized and confirmed in the church. But I went forward to make a public commitment, and something happened to me that night which changed my life. I became interested in spiritual things; I became interested in helping people. I had never done that before. I began to look at people in a totally different way than I had before.

You too can come to Christ. He will change your life. He will change the way you think. You will become a new creation.

32
Jesus the Water of Life

We need water to drink for our physical needs, but we also need spiritual water. Jesus said that the water he gives will become "a spring of water welling up to eternal life" (John 4:14, NIV).

God said, "My people have committed two sins; They have forsaken me, the spring of living water, and have dug their own cisterns, broken cisterns that cannot hold water" (Jeremiah 2:13, NIV). The Bible says, referring to people who have no spiritual water, "You will be… like a garden without water" (Isaiah 1:30, NIV).

There is a scarcity of spiritual water throughout the world. People are thirsty for spiritual water. We read about it constantly in our newspapers. We see people going to the wrong "watering holes," searching for satisfaction, searching for something that only the Water of life can satisfy. That Water of life is Jesus Christ.

Walk the streets of our major cities and you will see young people searching for something. They don't know what. Many people are searching for something, and they go after things—drink or sex or money—to try to quench their thirst. But whatever we do, it does not satisfy our spiritual thirst, the deepest longings of our hearts.

33
"I Want Some of That Hope!"

There is coming a day when Christ will return. He will come back with great glory and great power, with the armies of heaven, and nobody will be able to withstand his power. What a glorious hope we have as believers!

You say, "Well, what would I have to do to make sure that I am part of all this?" First, you have to repent of your sins. The word "repent" means to change. You have to say to God, "I have sinned and I'm sorry I've sinned." You must say, "I'm willing to change my whole way of living. I'm willing to change my lifestyle."

We must believe. Do you believe? You say, "Oh, sure, I believe. I have been going to church, and I believe in God and Christ and…" That is not what the word "believe" means. The word "believe" means you totally commit yourself to Jesus Christ as your Lord and Savior. You let him into your heart. You have a relationship with him personally through Bible reading and prayer and witnessing to others.

You must be willing to obey him from this moment on…. You are face to face with Christ who loves you, who died on the cross for you, who can forgive you, who can save you. He can give you new motivation; he can give you a purpose and a meaning for your life.

34
Be Sure to Hope in the Right Thing

On the purely human level there is little hope in the world. Immorality and lawlessness seem to be increasing. Wrong seems to be winning and right seems to be losing the battle for the minds and hearts of people. But the living Christ can bring glorious hope to individuals and to the world. Scripture says, "Blessed be the God and Father of our Lord Jesus Christ, which according to his abundant mercy hath begotten us again unto a lively hope by the resurrection of Jesus Christ from the dead" (1 Peter 1:3).

Many of us have put our faith in stocks, bonds, gadgets, pleasures, and thrills. Many of us have tried to bypass God. We are in trouble because we have left out God; we have left out the Ten Commandments; we have left out the Sermon on the Mount. Now we are reaping the tragic results. But in Christ there is hope for all.

All of us are facing death, and we can know that with Christ there is hope beyond the grave, because the same power that raised Christ from the dead will also raise those who confess him. Death becomes only a veil, only a river to cross; on the other side are heaven, home and Christ. One moment we say, "Good night," here, and the next, "Good morning," there.

35
The Crucified Christ

Jesus is the Crucified Christ. One Good Friday morning on television I saw people lashing themselves, thinking that by doing this they would please God. Some of them, as is their custom on Good Friday, had themselves tied to crosses. Some were even nailed to crosses. They believed that by doing that they could earn the pleasure of God and entrance to heaven.

No. Jesus did it all on the cross. He bowed his head and said, "It is finished" (John 19:30). We can do good works, we can have ourselves nailed to a thousand crosses, but that won't get us to heaven. What will get us to heaven is what Jesus did on that cross that day at Calvary when he shed his blood for us.

Why did Jesus die? Not because he had sinned. He died in our place. The Scripture says, "For he hath made him to be sin for us, who knew no sin; that we might be made the righteousness of God in him" (2 Corinthians 5:21). Think of it. He was made sin. He became guilty of adultery, of murder, of lying, of envy, of jealousy. He took all our sin on him. Because Jesus did that, God says, "I can forgive you."

36
The Contemporary Christ

Jesus is also the Contemporary Christ. I received a letter from a man who was reared in a good family. He wrote, "I always thought I was a Christian. But my first weeks at the university proved to me that my religion was more external than internal, and I set it all aside. I was successful on my chosen path. Then I received a glimmer of revelation. It was that if Jesus Christ is the Son of God, as he claims, I'm a fool not to follow him. In the years since, Jesus has consistently demonstrated to me, to my wife, and to our children the magnificent truth of his words: 'I am the light of the world; he who follows me will not walk in darkness, but will have the light of life'" (John 8:12, RSV).

Has that been your discovery? Do you know Christ?

Rousing dockside welcome home from five-month European crusade, July 1954.

37
The Coming Christ

Jesus is also the Coming Christ. Jesus said, "I will come again" (John 14:3).

Who can solve the problems of the world? The Bible teaches that Jesus Christ is the "Prince of Peace" (Isaiah 9:6). He is coming back and bringing peace some day. He is coming back to save us from bombing ourselves off this planet. He will establish his kingdom of peace and prosperity.

Our hope in Christ. You can know him. Christ died for you. He rose again. He loves you. He wants to help you. He has arms outstretched toward you—to love you, to help you, and to forgive you. But you must do something. You must repent of your sins…. Then you must receive him by faith. If you wait until you can understand it all intellectually, you will never come. The Scripture says that by wisdom people cannot know God (see 1 Corinthians 1:21). You come with your mind, you come with your heart, but primarily you come with your will. Say, "I will surrender to him. I will serve him. I will follow him. I will turn from my sins and receive him into my heart by faith." Commit your life to him today.

38
Hope for Whomsoever

The angel at Christ's birth spoke "to all people" (Luke 2:10). Christ's redemption isn't for a chosen race, a select class or a particular group. It is offered to all people. There is no suggestion or implication that God has favorites of class, race or nation. The Bible indicates that to God people are divided into two classes: believers and unbelievers. John 3:16 bears that out: "For God so loved the world, that he gave his only begotten Son, that whosoever believeth in him should not perish, but have everlasting life" (John 3:16). That word "whosoever" embraces the whole world. "All have sinned" (see Romans 3:23, 5:12), therefore, all need the Savior. The Bible says, "Unto you is born this day... a Savior" (Luke 2:11). That is part of the good tidings. It is for all people.

The sad thing is that even now, almost 2,000 years after his birth, many of the earth's people have not heard the Good News and, consequently, do not know the joy of his salvation.

39

Don't Let Time Be Your Tyrant

Time can be a tyrant. It controls us, and we become frustrated, running from one thing to another because we do not feel that we have enough time to get everything done that needs to be done. In the Lord's work there is so little time, and so much to do!

If we could only be like the Lord Jesus, who moved with such serenity! He never seemed to be in a hurry, yet he only had three years of ministry. Jesus said, "As long as it is day, we must do the work of him who sent me. Night is coming, when no one can work" (John 9:4, NIV).

Jesus taught us that quality of life is more important than length of life. To the world, when he was on the cross, he must have seemed a failure. People still needed to be healed, and hungry people still needed to be fed. Yet at the end of his life he said, "I have finished the work which thou gavest me to do" (John 17:4).

You may not live long, but finish the work God gave you to do. That is the important thing—not to live a long time—but to have a quality of life every day in prayer, the study of the Word, witnessing, bearing the fruit of the Spirit, utilizing the gifts of the Spirit.

40

Thanking Our Friends and Thanking God

Thanksgiving is a part of the most intimate relationship between us and God. Yet there are thousands today who are not thankful. We aren't thankful as individuals, nor are we thankful as a nation.

It is the custom of many Christians to bow their heads and give thanks for the food that has been placed before them. I have had scores of waiters and waitresses tell me that when our family bowed our heads, it was the first time that they had ever seen that happen in their restaurants.

Thanksgiving is a recognition of debt that cannot be repaid. We express thanks when we are not able to reimburse the giver. When thanksgiving is filled with true meaning and is not just the formality of a polite "thank you," it is the recognition of dependence. Because we are in debt to our friends, we thank them for doing for us what we desired or needed. But because of the pride and arrogance of our hearts, we take from God without even the formality of thanksgiving, not acknowledging how deeply indebted we are to him.

41
"I wish God would be more personal."

The Hebrew prophets such as Isaiah, Jeremiah, and Ezekiel not only believed in God but they worshiped Him. They believed that God could be seen in nature. They believed that he had made the world. But all through the centuries they seem to have been saying, "I wish that God would become personal."

This is precisely what he did that first Christmas night. He became personal in Bethlehem. "The Word was made flesh, and dwelt among us. No man hath seen God at any time; the only begotten Son, which is in the bosom of the Father, he hath declared him" (John 1:14, 18). At a specific time and at a specific place a specific Person was born and that Person was God of very God, the Lord Jesus Christ.

From the lips of Jesus came these words: "The Son of man is come to seek and to save that which was lost" (Luke 19:10). Like piercing trumpets these words herald the breaking in of the Divine into human history. What a wonderful and glorious hope we have because of that first Christmas!

42
A Teenager Named Mary

One evening in Jerusalem I looked out of my hotel window and saw the lights of Bethlehem in the distance. For a long time I stood there and meditated on the events that had taken place nearly 2,000 years ago which have transformed our world.

I thought about the angel Gabriel. He came to Mary, who was no more than a teenager, and said, "Fear not, Mary: for thou hast found favor with God. And, behold, thou shalt conceive in thy womb, and bring forth a son, and shalt call his name Jesus" (Luke 1:30-33)....

Mary showed one of the most remarkable demonstrations of faith found in the Bible. Here she was, a virgin, engaged to a godly man by the name of Joseph, yet she was to be made pregnant supernaturally by the Holy Spirit. People would talk, shame would be attached to it, and Joseph would probably leave her. But Mary by faith said, "Behold the handmaid of the Lord; be it unto me according to thy word" (Luke 1:38).

Scripture says, "Faith is the substance of things hoped for, the evidence of things not seen," then lists the great heroes of faith (Hebrews 11). But I believe that one of the greatest demonstrations of faith in all the Bible was Mary's answer to the angel in accepting God's will for her life, no matter what the cost.

43
Shepherds, Not Scholars, Heard of Him First

One of the greatest sermons ever preached was delivered by an angel on the first Christmas night: "And there were in the same country shepherds abiding in the field, keeping watch over their flock by night. And, lo, the angel of the Lord came upon them, and the glory of the Lord shone round about them: and they were sore afraid. And the angel said unto them, Fear not: for, behold, I bring you good tidings of great joy, which shall be to all people. For unto you is born this day in the city of David a Savior, which is Christ the Lord" (Luke 2:8-11).

The first Christmas worship service was conducted not in a temple, or in a cathedral, or in a synagogue, but in the great out-of-doors. The tidings of Christ's birth echoed in the skies. The angel of the Lord proclaimed the good news to lowly shepherds. The shepherds, though poor, could discern the voice from heaven above the noisy din of earth's confusion. Strange that this glad word was not first given to the priests or the scholars or the Pharisees. God speaks to those who are prepared in their hearts to listen.

44

His Eyes of Compassion Are on Us

Because of his holiness, God cannot condone sin, but he loves the sinner and has made provision to forgive sin through the atonement of his Son: "God commendeth his love toward us, in that, while we were yet sinners, Christ died for us" (Romans 5:8)....

God's eyes of compassion have been following us as we have stumbled through history under the burden of our own wretchedness. Yet Calvary should prove even to the most skeptical that God is not blind to our plight, but that he was willing to suffer with us. The word "compassion" comes from two Latin words meaning "to suffer with." God's all-consuming love for mankind was best demonstrated at the cross, where his compassion was embodied in Jesus Christ. "God was in Christ, reconciling the world unto himself" (2 Corinthians 5:19).

Jeremiah the prophet wrote, "The Lord hath appeared of old unto me, saying, Yea, I have loved thee with an everlasting love: therefore with lovingkindness have I drawn thee" (Jeremiah 31:3). The Apostle Paul spoke of "God, who is rich in mercy, for his great love wherewith he loved us" (Ephesians 2:4). It was the love of God that sent Jesus Christ to the cross.

45

In Your Loneliness, Reach Out to God

Our reaction to loneliness is often to deal with the symptoms rather than the cause. We become involved in pleasures, parties, good times, sex. We become involved in our work. We throw ourselves into the social whirl.

Any attempt to deal with sin without conversion is like struggling in quicksand. How many people today are trying to save themselves but can't! If you have come to the end of your rope, turn your life over to Christ. Let him bear your burdens, help you solve your problems, direct and lead you in your life. Jesus Christ restores our most fundamental relationship in life: "Behold, I stand at the door and knock: if anyone hears my voice and opens the door, I will come in to him, and dine with him, and he with me" (Revelation 3:20, NKJV). But you have to make this decision alone.

The psalmist said, "O my soul, why be so gloomy and discouraged? Trust in God. I shall yet praise him for his wondrous help. He will make me smile again, for he is my God" (see Psalms 42:5). Often loneliness is God's way of letting us know that it is time to reach out. Reach out to the cross and say, "Lord, I open my heart and my life to You. I commit myself to You."

46
Redeem Your Time for God

One reason we should "number our days" and "apply our hearts unto wisdom" (Psalms 90:12) is that the day is lost which does not add to our knowledge of God and his Word. In eternity's scale of values that day is lost which has no word of praise, no prayer of thanks ,and no contact with God. Prayer and praise are not occasional notes played on the organ of life; they are pipes in the organ, and their absence means serious loss to the music of life. It means discord instead of harmony.

Likewise, to most of us the Scriptures are an untapped treasure. This mine of spiritual gold lies unopened and unused, while we exist in spiritual poverty. Job said, "I have esteemed the words of his mouth more than my necessary food" (Job 23:12).

How small a segment of eternity is this brief period called time! And yet we squander it so foolishly, with little or no thought of eternity.

47
Redeem Your Time for Your Friends

Another reason we are to "number our days" and "apply our hearts unto wisdom" (Psalms 90:12) is that we should find in our hearts a desire to live outgoing, outflowing lives in the context not of time but of eternity. We should live Spirit-filled lives, lives directed by the Holy Spirit, lives of daily victory.

We should take time to be pleasant and to smile. I've found all over the world that people of all races and cultures respond to a smile. There is so much unpleasantness in this world, but the Bible says, "The kingdom of God is... peace, and joy" (Romans 14:17); and, "The fruit of the Spirit is love, joy, peace" (Galatians 5:22).

The small courtesies which we often omit because we believe that they are of no value will some day seem larger to us than the wealth and the fame for which we struggle so hard. Take time to show love to your family. Counselors tell us that most people who come to them are starved for love. Let us take time for the good-bye kiss; we will go to work with a sweeter spirit.

48
Redeem Your Time for Your Family

Let us take time to get acquainted with our families. All the wealth which we are accumulating is no substitute to our children whom we have no time to caress. We are not machines; we are not robots. The art of living and the secret of a happy home is for the members of the family to learn to give and to receive love. When we are gone, our families will remember us not for our business sense, or for our wealth, or for our cleverness, but for our love: "Now abideth faith, hope, and love; but the greatest, and the most abiding, is love" (see 1 Corinthians 13:13).

Let us take time for family devotions. Too many families have left all matters of religion to the church; but the greatest, the most lasting, lessons of faith are learned when a mother's or a father's voice is lifted in reverent prayer to God. Prayer together at the close of the day will make sleep come easier and will absolve the little hurts and harsh words of the day.

49
"I Am the Light of the World."

Jesus said, "I am the light of the world." We may not understand exactly what light is, but we do know its effects. We know that there could be no plant or animal or human life on this earth without light. What the sun is to the earth, Jesus Christ is to the human heart: "I am the light of the world: he that followeth me shall not walk in darkness, but shall have the light of life" (John 8:12).

Many of you have been groping your way through life. You have been stumbling and faltering as if you were in darkness. Many of you have been confirmed in the church. You have been baptized. But deep in your hearts you don't have the satisfaction, the peace and assurance that Christ is in you. Christ wants to bring his light into your hearts.

But Jesus said something else: "You are the light of the world" (Matthew 5:14, RSV). We are to be as lights. When we reflect the light of Jesus, we become lights. Right in our community, wherever we work or wherever we live, we can be lights.

People will look at us and see the fruit of the Spirit in our lives, and they will begin to ask: "What makes her different? Why is he different?"

We can tell them, "Christ makes the difference."

50
"I Am the Good Shepherd."

Jesus said, "I am the good shepherd" (John 10:11). We are sheep, he is the Shepherd. The shepherd lives with his sheep. He gives them food and protection and security. Sheep cannot survive without a shepherd. Without a shepherd, sheep fall prey to wolves and wild dogs and thieves, and they wander and become lost. We possess many of the characteristics of sheep, because sheep are shortsighted and tend to stray. Scripture says, "All we like sheep have gone astray; we have [each turned] to his own way" (Isaiah 53:6).

Jesus said, "The sheep know their Master's voice.... He calls them by name" (see John 10:3-4). Jesus, the Good Shepherd, knows you by name. We are to be like sheep following him.

At great personal sacrifice at the cross the Good Shepherd sought the lost sheep. We were the lost sheep. He went to the cross for us. He said, "I lay down my life for the sheep" (John 10:15). To those who follow him, Jesus said, "I am with you always, even unto the end of the world" (Matthew 28:20).

51
"I Am the Resurrection, and the Life."

Jesus said, "I am the resurrection, and the life: he that believeth in me, though he were dead, yet shall he live" (John 11:25). Why should people say that we cannot rise from the dead? Which is more difficult, to be born or to rise from the dead? Have you ever seen a baby born? I saw my last son born. And the doctor, who was not a Christian, said to me, "How can anyone watch a scene like this and still be an atheist?" Think of all that is involved in the birth of a baby and how that baby is a little life in the hands of God. There is a soul inside that little body.

I believe that after I die, I will rise. I don't know exactly how God will do it. I don't know exactly what my form will be, but I am looking forward to that day. We are told that there will be a resurrection and that those who have died, even centuries ago, will be raised from the dead.

And we will see Christ. I believe that when we die, the time from our death to the moment of our resurrection is quick, and then we will be in the presence of Christ. What a wonderful hope that gives us!

Winding up his New York Crusade at the Polo Grounds, October 1957.

52
"I Am the Way, the Truth, and the Life."

Jesus said, "I am the way, the truth, and the life: no man cometh unto the Father, but by me" (John 14:6). That was what I wondered about when I was thinking about accepting Christ as my Lord and Savior. When I came to Christ, I thought, "Here is a man who says, 'I am the embodiment of all truth'—all scientific truth, all psychological truth, all philosophical truth—'I am... the truth.' Is he crazy? Is he lying? Maybe he is who he claims to be!" I had to make a decision.

So I said, "Lord, I believe You. I believe that You are the way, the truth, and the life, and that no one comes to the Father but by You." And I repented of my sins and received him into my heart.

You need to say, "I need Christ in my life." You need to know that Christ lives in your heart, and you must make a decision about that. You can invite Christ into your heart right now.

53
Nailed to the Cross by His Love

The nails driven into Christ's hands and feet by Roman soldiers could not hold him there. That day there were other nails, invisible nails, which caused him to stay on the cross when he could have come down from it: The first invisible nail was the nail of love....

In a world of hatred, God gave his Son to be born in Bethlehem. Hatred pursued Christ. After Jesus' birth, Herod, full of hatred, sent out a decree that all children two years old and under who lived in and near Bethlehem were to be destroyed.

The Pharisees hated Jesus because the truth of his Gospel brought their hypocrisy to light. The high priests hated him because his popularity with the multitudes threatened to lure people away from established religious ritual. The Romans hated him because his philosophy of love and nonresistance drew followers....

The world had never seen such a manifestation of selfless love as was demonstrated on Calvary. The world had no ability to comprehend it. It was this nail of divine love which held Christ to the cross. Such unselfish love should inspire deep gratitude in us, produce submissiveness to the Savior, and prompt us to live for the One who died for us.

54
Nailed to the Cross by His Loyalty

The second invisible nail which held Jesus to the cross was the nail of loyalty.

Jesus lived in the shadow of the cross. As a boy, he spoke of his Father's business. As a man, he referred to his sacrificial work upon the cross. His sayings were filled with allusions to his impending death on the cross. His whole ministry pointed like an arrow to Golgotha and to the fulfillment of the divine purpose for his life. He said, "As Moses lifted up the serpent in the wilderness, even so must the Son of man be lifted up" (John 3:14)....

Jesus died upon Golgotha in a supreme demonstration of loyalty to God's will, but the unbelieving world has forgotten that 2,000-year-old scene of Calvary. The world will believe the redemption story of Christ as they see the power of the cross demonstrated in your life and in mine.

Christ's loyalty to Calvary should inspire us to be loyal to the cross, to "take up our cross" (see Matthew 16:24) and to follow him. Then will the world be reminded of Calvary and, because of our Christ-honoring lives, will be drawn to believe in the Christ.

55
Nailed to the Cross by Our Sin

The third invisible nail which held Jesus to the cross was the nail of sin. Isaiah wrote much about the sacrificial ministry of Christ: "Surely he hath borne our griefs, and carried our sorrows: yet we did esteem him stricken, smitten of God, and afflicted. But he was wounded for our transgressions, he was bruised for our iniquities" (Isaiah 53:4-5).

Had there been no sin in the world, there would have been no need for the cross....

The wooden cross upon which Christ died was a tangible symbol that we had been at cross-purposes with God, and it was because of the existence of our sin, our cross-purposes with the will of God, that Jesus died. It was the nail of sin which held him there.

It was not only universal sin which held Jesus to the cross—it was my sin and your sin. If our sins are not responsible for Calvary, then Calvary has no responsibility for our sins. God, knowing the hearts of all men and women, and knowing that they were only evil continually, offered his Son to die for all people: those living, and those yet unborn.

Calvary is the place of decision. It is the eternal divider, erected to separate people into two classes: the saved and the lost. Embrace its truth and be saved. Reject it and be lost.

56
Grace for the Thief Means Grace for Us

At Calvary a man was dying who deserved hell. He was a thief. He was a murderer. Yet in the last moment he turned to Christ and said, "Lord, remember me" (Luke 23:42). In that moment Jesus turned to him and said, "Today shalt thou be with me in Paradise" (Luke 23:43).

I expect to see that man in Paradise. That man is in heaven today. Not because he could come down from the cross and be baptized. Not because he could come down from the cross and take communion. Not because he could come down from the cross and give money to charitable work. Not because he could come down from the cross and live a good life. He had been a wicked, godless man, but he was saved by the tender mercy and grace of God.

And that is what brings us to the cross. You will never understand what the cross means until you understand in your own life the assurance that God gives us in his Word: "By grace are ye saved through faith; and that not of yourselves: it is the gift of God" (Ephesians 2:8).

57
His Resurrection Dispels Doubt

What significance did Christ's resurrection have for his disciples? What bearing did it have on the future of Christianity?

First, the resurrection dispelled all doubts. Those who had not made contact with the living Lord, those who did not know him and the power of his resurrection naturally had doubts. Remember Thomas? That Christ should have risen was inconceivable to him: "Except I shall see in his hands the print of the nails,... I will not believe" (John 20:25).

How did Thomas triumph over his doubts? He did not do it by speculation but by a revelation. Jesus appeared to him and said, "Reach hither thy finger, and behold my hands;... and be not faithless, but believing" (John 20:27). It was in the sublimity of that personal relationship with the living Lord that Thomas said, "My Lord and my God" (John 20:28). Belief comes when you enter into an intimate, personal relationship with the Christ of Easter. To stand in the presence of a resurrected, glorified Savior, resplendent with the radiance of another world, is to repeat the word of that believing disciple: "My Lord and my God!"

58
His Resurrection Dissipates Fear

Second, Christ's resurrection dissipated fear. The Bible says, "And if Christ be not raised, your faith is vain" (1 Corinthians 15:17). Faith cannot exist in dead, lifeless matter. All of the hopes of that little band of believers were locked up in the tomb of Joseph of Arimathea with the linen-wrapped body of their Lord. Implicit faith had given way to stark fear. The Bible says, "The doors were shut where the disciples were assembled for fear" (John 20:19).

We live in a world which is shaken by fear, apprehension, and anxiety. The farther we get from the fact of the resurrection, the closer we get to the fear of destruction. The words "Christ or chaos" have come to be more than clever alliteration. They express an alternative which we must act upon.

Individuals are locked in prisons of fear. Nations tremble in the grip of collective fear. Cities are held in the dire clutch of fear. What is the answer to this stifling fear?

The fear of those first disciples disappeared when they found themselves in the presence of their living Lord. The words, "Be not afraid" (Matthew 28:10), will dispel fear in any century. The answer to individual fear is a personal faith in a living, glorified Lord.

59

His Resurrection Defeats Death

Third, Christ's resurrection meant that death's decree had been broken. The Bible says, "For as in Adam all die, even so in Christ shall all be made alive" (1 Corinthians 15:22). For centuries death held mankind in its viselike grip. But around the opened door of Christ's empty tomb bloomed the lilies of immortality. The words "Because I live, ye shall live also" (John 14:19) negated death's decree and opened the gates of a blissful eternity for everyone who is clothed in the garments of everlasting life through faith in his name.

Paul sang triumphantly, "O death, where is thy sting? O grave, where is thy victory?" (1 Corinthians 15:55). We are told that many of the disciples paid the supreme sacrifice upon the altar of devotion for the love of their Lord. Fresh in their minds were the words of their Savior: "I am the resurrection, and the life: he that believeth in me, though he were dead, yet shall he live" (John 11:25).

60
His Resurrection Ends Loneliness

Fourth, Christ's resurrection is the answer to loneliness. Some of you are suffocated by a depressing loneliness. But God did not create you to live in unbearable solitude. God was the first to realize that it is not good for us to live alone. Christ, through his life, death, and resurrection, provided an effective cure for the loneliness of mankind. Not only to the disciples but to everyone of every age he said, "Lo, I am with you always, even unto the end of the world" (Matthew 28:20)....

The two disciples who walked sadly along the Emmaus road were symbolic of all of the lonely people who have never known the living Lord. Jesus said, "What manner of communications are these that ye have one to another, as ye walk, and are sad?" (Luke 24:17). But after they had touched him personally and experienced the power of his presence, they asked, "Did not our heart burn within us, while he talked with us by the way, and while he opened to us the scriptures?" (Luke 24:32). Their loneliness was dispelled by the resurrected Christ.

Earth has no balm that can cure the loneliness of the human spirit. Our souls cry out for fellowship with God, and Christ alone can fill this longing of our hearts.

61
His Resurrection Brings Forgiveness

Fifth, Christ's resurrection means that we are not in our sins anymore. The Bible says, "If Christ be not raised, your faith is vain; ye are still in your sins" (1 Corinthians 15:17). Paul, who wrote those words, had declared, "But ye are washed, but ye are sanctified, but ye are justified in the name of the Lord Jesus, and by the Spirit of our God" (1 Corinthians 6:11). Again and again he made statements like this: "There is therefore now no condemnation to them which are in Christ Jesus" (Romans 8:1).

I tell you with all the authority of the Word of God that every person who puts his trust in Christ can become a partaker of eternal life. When we do, the moment we die our soul goes into eternity to live with Christ forever. The Bible says that someday the bodies of the dead in Christ shall rise, and we shall ever be with the Lord.

Because Jesus was raised from the dead, our loneliness is conquered, our fears dispelled, and our sins forgiven; we are on our way to heaven. We have access to God in Christ.

62
Napoleon Didn't Know It Was Easter!

As Easter bells in churches and cathedrals around the world sound, not the death knell of Christ but the victorious chime of the living Lord, those glad words, "He is risen," come freshly to believing hearts everywhere.

During Napoleon's Austrian campaign his army advanced to within six miles of Feldkirch. It looked as though Bonaparte's men would take Feldkirch without resistance. But as they advanced toward their objective in the night, the Christians of Feldkirch gathered in a little church to pray. It was Easter Eve.

The next morning at sunrise the bells of the village pealed out across the countryside. Napoleon's army, not realizing it was Easter Sunday, thought that in the night the Austrian army had moved into Feldkirch and that the bells were ringing in jubilation. Napoleon ordered a retreat, and the battle at Feldkirch never took place. The Easter bells caused the enemy to retreat, and peace reigned in the Austrian countryside.

At Eastertime you may be surrounded by enemies which storm the citadel of your soul. The Easter bells, when you realize their full significance, cause the threatening forces to retreat.

63

My Decision at Forest Home

The Word of God never changes. Early in my life I had some doubts about the Word, but one night in 1949 I knelt before a stump in the woods near Forest Home, California. I opened my Bible and I said, "O God, there are many things in this Book I do not understand, but I accept it by faith as Your infallible Word from Genesis to Revelation." I settled that, and from that moment on I have never had a single doubt that this is God's Word. So when I quote the Bible, when I preach it, I know that I am preaching the truth of God.

This gives authority to one's ministry. It is not based on what someone says about the Bible. It is not based on some book I have read. It is based on faith in God. You cannot change that. You cannot move that.

64
That Sounds Like the United States!

I was on an airplane one day, and sitting beside me was a sociology professor. I happened to be reading the third chapter of Second Timothy. He asked to see what I was reading, so I gave him this passage to read:

"You must realize that in the last days the times will be full of danger. Men will become utterly self-centered, greedy for money, full of big words. They will be proud and contemptuous, without any regard for what their parents taught them. They will be utterly lacking in gratitude, purity, and normal human affections.... They will be passionate and unprincipled, treacherous, self-willed and conceited, loving... what gives them pleasure instead of loving God. They will maintain a facade of 'religion,' but their conduct will deny its validity" (2 Timothy 3:1-5, Phillips).

When he finished reading, he turned to me and said, "You know, that is a description of our country today."

I replied, "Yes, and that was written 2,000 years ago."

With singer Ethel Waters, June 1976

65

Four Steps to Mending a Fractured Family

Thousands of homes are almost on the rocks. Many couples are fearful lest their marriages break some day. You have one great insurance policy that can guarantee the unity and happiness of your home.

Make Christ the center of your home. A home is like a solar system. The center, the great sun, holds the solar system together. If it were not for the sun, our solar system would fly to pieces. And unless the Son of God is at the center of your home, it too may fly to pieces. Make the Son of God the center of your home.

Attend church regularly. See to it that your entire family is faithful in Sunday school and church attendance, and that it is integrated into the various activities of the church.

Be certain that there is loving Christian discipline in the home. Obedience of children to parents is a virtue. The most effective way for parents to deserve obedience is by a clean, pure, wholesome, Christian example.

Establish daily family devotions. Offer a prayer of thanksgiving at each meal. Have a special time in the morning or evening when the entire family gathers to read the Bible and to pray.

66
The Adults Came to Children's Church!

When I quote the Scriptures, I know I am quoting the Word of God. It is God's authoritative message to us. It is an infallible Book.

We need to saturate ourselves in the Word of God and in prayer. One reason people listened to Jesus was that he spoke as one having authority.

A friend of mine who is a pastor decided that he would have a service for children at 8:30 on Sunday mornings. He spoke using simple words, illustrating his message with graphs and diagrams. In about a year more older people were coming to the 8:30 service than to the regular service at 10:30 because they could understand what he was talking about. People want simplicity. I believe that was one of the secrets of our Lord. The common people heard him gladly. He spoke their language.

Professor James Denny, of Scotland, once said that Jesus probably repeated himself more than 500 times. In college I had a professor who repeated himself three times. He said that the people in the first two or three rows will get it the first time. The second time the people in the middle will get it. The third time the people in the back will get it. And the ones in the front row will never forget it.

67
Peace With God

Jesus Christ came to reverse the effects of the Fall. He brings peace with God, peace to the human heart and peace between persons....

The Bible speaks of peace with God. Jesus Christ has made it possible for rebellious humans to be reconciled to God through his atoning death on the cross and his resurrection. "Therefore," the Bible says, "being justified by faith, we have peace with God through our Lord Jesus Christ" (Romans 5:1).

From God's point of view we are already at war with him. We need reconciliation; we need peace with God. Christ alone can change the human heart.

Where does war come from? How did it start? The first war was when Cain killed Abel. Why? Because sin was in Cain's heart. The book of James answers the question of where war comes from: "Come they not hence, even of your lusts that war in your members?" (James 4:1). That is why human solutions alone cannot solve in any lasting way the problems we face in our world. Only Christ can deal with our deepest problem. The deepest problem we face is the spiritual problem of the human heart that needs to be reconciled to God and forgiven of its sin.

68
The Peace of God

The Bible also speaks of the peace of God. That is the peace which God can bring to the human heart. Jesus promised, "Peace I leave with you, my peace I give unto you: not as the world giveth, give I unto you. Let not your heart be troubled, neither let it be afraid" (John 14:27)....

Perhaps you are searching for peace; you are longing for it. You thought that you would find it if you made a lot of money, but you didn't find it. You thought that you would find it if you had sexual experiences, but you didn't find it.

You thought that you would find it through drink, but you didn't find it. You thought that you would find it in getting and accumulating vast knowledge, but you didn't find it. You've searched the religions of the world, but you haven't found peace.

There are a thousand ways that you have turned, trying to find peace, but you have not found it. You may escape from reality for a few moments, for a few hours, but then the old burden comes back. The old suffering, the old emptiness, the old monotony, the old grind, returns.

Give your life to Christ, and let him give you "the peace of God, which passeth all understanding" (Philippians 4:7).

69
Peace on Earth

The Bible also speaks of peace among men and women on earth. God can give peace in our homes, peace in our towns and villages and nations.

When Adam and Eve sinned against God, their relationship with God was broken. But in addition, their relationship with each other was broken. Since that time, the effects of the Fall have shattered relationships on every level—husband against wife, brother against brother, neighbor against neighbor, tribe against tribe, nation against nation. It has always been that way. But Christ came to reconcile us to God, and when he returns, he will bring peace and justice to the whole world....

We must be concerned with human suffering wherever it is found, because God is concerned about it. We must be concerned with the larger issues of strife between nations, especially the issue of peace in this nuclear age. God is concerned about these things.

70
Let's Do It All in Jesus' Name!

We Christians will do what we can to help the poor, to heal the sick, to feed the hungry, to see that justice is done. But we must never forget that how or when a person dies is less important than where he or she will spend eternity. If you feed all the hungry, care for all the poor, heal all the sick, yet fail to explain God's way of salvation to them, you have not reached their deepest need. Their deepest need is spiritual. Let us give, but give in Jesus' name. Let us feed, but feed in Jesus' name. Let us heal, but heal in Jesus' name. Let us teach, but teach in Jesus' name. And let us dedicate ourselves to work for peace, in Jesus' name.

71
Give Your Best Time to Your Children

Take time with your children. I heard about a father who gave his son an unusual Christmas present. He wrapped a note inside a package. The note read: "Son, during the next year I am going to give you one hour every day and two hours on Sunday." The boy put his arms around his dad and said, "That's the best Christmas present I've ever had."

Your children not only require a great deal of your time, but they long and hunger for it. Perhaps they do not express it, but the hunger and the longing are there just the same. Be a friend to your children, love them, spend hours with them.

Cut out some of your "important social engagements," and make your home the center of your social life. God will honor you, and your children will grow up to call you "blessed" (see Proverbs 31:28).

72

Give Your Best Example to Your Children

Set your children a good example. A well-known story illustrates this point: It was the usual custom for a lawyer who walked to his office to stop at the corner tavern for a drink. One day, when the snow had fallen, he heard a sound behind him. Turning, he saw his seven-year-old son stretching as far as he could to step into his father's tracks in the new-fallen snow.

The father asked, "Son, what are you doing?" The son replied, "I'm stepping in your tracks." The father sent his son home, but he couldn't go to the tavern; all he could think of was a son stepping in his father's tracks.

When he was studying his law case that day, the boy's words kept returning, "I'm stepping in your tracks." That father got down on his knees and accepted Christ as his Savior and Lord. He said, "From now on I want my son to step in the tracks of a Christian father."

Many parents preach to their children, but do not set good examples. Parents want the children to do as they say, not as they do.

73
The Innkeeper's Response

What was the response of the innkeeper, when Mary and Joseph wanted to find a room where Christ could be born? The innkeeper was not hostile; he was not opposed to them; but his inn was crowded; his hands were full; his mind was preoccupied (see Luke 2:7).

He probably told them, "I wish I could help you, but I must keep my priorities. After all, this is a business, and this coming Child is no real concern of mine, but I'm not a hardhearted man. Over there is the stable. You are welcome to use it if you care to, but that is the best I can do. Now I must get back to my work. My guests are needing me."

And this is the answer that millions are giving today. It is the answer of preoccupation—not fierce opposition, not furious hatred, but unconcern about spiritual things. Secular priorities, even at Christmastime, occupy first place.

74
A Second Chance in Football, and Life

Georgia Tech played the University of California in the 1929 Rose Bowl. In the game a player recovered a fumble, but became confused and ran the wrong way. A teammate tackled him just before he would have scored a touchdown against his own team. At halftime all of the players went into the dressing room and sat down, wondering what the coach would say. This young man sat by himself, put a towel over his head, and cried.

When the team was ready to go back onto the field for the second half, the coach stunned the team when he announced that the same players who had started the first half would start the second. All of the players left the dressing room except this young man. He would not budge. The coach looked back as he called him again, and saw that his cheeks were wet with tears. The player said, "Coach, I can't do it. I've ruined you. I've disgraced the University of California. I can't face that crowd in the stadium again."

Then the coach put his hand on the player's shoulder and said, "Get up and go back in. The game is only half over."

When I think of that story, deep inside I say, "What a coach!" When I read the story of Jonah, and the stories of thousands like him, I say, "To think that God would give me another chance!"

75
In Moldavia: Bible Pictures on Barns

We are all slaves of sin, and Christ came to set us free from that slavery.

When we were in Romania we visited the principality of Moldavia. What a beautiful part of Romania that is! The bishop took us on a trip around Moldavia, and we saw those famous buildings, barns, and houses with paintings on them. They were all scriptural paintings. In the old days when they didn't have literature, they drew pictures from the Bible on barns and taught the Bible from those paintings. One picture I will never forget. It is of a stairway to heaven, and pilgrims are going up the ladder. Below them are devils trying to pull them down into the flames of hell. At the top of the picture Jesus is standing, waiting for them. Also at the top are angels helping the pilgrims along. That shows the great battle that we all face between good and evil, between God and Satan....

Scripture teaches that we must make this choice ourselves. Our parents can't make this decision for us. We must make the great decision of total surrender to the Lordship of Christ.

76
"Dr. Livingstone, I Presume?"

To serve Christ is costly. Jesus said, "Count the cost" (see Luke 14:28).

Nearly 200 years ago there were two Scottish brothers named John and David Livingstone. John had set his mind on making money and becoming wealthy, and he did. But under his name in an old edition of the "Encyclopaedia Britannica" John Livingstone is listed simply as "the brother of David Livingstone."

And who was David Livingstone? While John had dedicated himself to making money, David had knelt and prayed. Surrendering himself to Christ, he resolved, "I will place no value on anything I have or possess unless it is in relationship to the Kingdom of God." The inscription over his burial place in Westminster Abbey reads, "For thirty years his life was spent in an unwearied effort to evangelize."

On his 59th birthday David Livingstone wrote, "My Jesus, my King, my Life, my All; I again dedicate my whole self to Thee."

77
Five Things I Know About My Audience

There are five things I know about any audience to which I speak. First, I know that life's needs are not totally met by social improvement or material affluence.... Some of the most heartsick people I know are millionaires.

Second, I know that there is an essential emptiness in every life without Christ. Many millions today are crying for something, but nothing seems to satisfy. Money doesn't satisfy. Sensual experiences do not satisfy. God, only God, satisfies....

Third, I know that people are lonely. A friend of mine at an American university is both a psychologist and a theologian. On one occasion I asked him, "What is the greatest problem of the patients who come to you for help?" He thought for a moment and replied, "Loneliness... loneliness for God."...

Fourth, I know that people have a devastating sense of guilt. The head of a psychiatric hospital told me, "I could release half my patients if I could find a way to get rid of their sense of guilt." ...

Fifth, I know that there is a universal fear of death. A survey reported that although young people think about sex more than any other subject, the second thing they think about most is death.

Isaiah's Experience: Comprehension

Isaiah tells us of his call to be a prophet: "I heard the voice of the Lord, saying, 'Whom shall I send, and who will go for us?' Then said I, 'Here am I; send me.' And [the Lord] said, 'Go, and tell this people...'" (Isaiah 6:8-9). Isaiah's experience should be our experience:

First, Isaiah *comprehended* who God is.... The ultimate experience of life is knowing God. The Apostle Paul said, "I consider everything a loss compared to the surpassing greatness of knowing Christ Jesus my Lord" (Philippians 3:8, NIV). Isaiah comprehended God and saw him in his righteousness and holiness. And he saw the seraphim, and they were crying, "Holy, holy, holy, is the Lord of hosts: the whole earth is full of his glory" (Isaiah 6:3). The seraphim were recognizing the holiness and righteousness of God.

Scripture tells us that unless we have that same righteousness and that same holiness, we will never get to heaven. We must have it, and we don't have it except in Christ. When Christ died on the cross, he provided us with a righteousness and a holiness and a goodness that we don't have on our own, and we are clothed in the righteousness of God. When God sees us, he sees the righteousness of Christ and he doesn't condemn us.

79
Isaiah's Experience: Conviction

As soon as Isaiah saw who God really is, his response was a deep *conviction* of his own sinfulness. He said, "Woe is me! for I am undone; because I am a man of unclean lips" (Isaiah 6:5).

The closer we are to Christ, the more sinful and unworthy we will feel. The fact that we are aware of our sin and feel guilty about it is a sign of spiritual life....

A lot of what goes on today in Christian circles indicates that we have not really comprehended and experienced God as Isaiah did. We have arrived at the point where we are flippant about God. We tell jokes about him. God's name is used so often in profanity in the entertainment world that sometimes it is embarrassing to watch television.

We do not realize how this offends a holy and righteous God. We act as if it doesn't matter how we live or what we think or say. We have moved in with the world, and we have allowed the world to penetrate the way we live. So the things that we used to call sin no longer seem to be sin to us. As I pray, I find myself confessing things that the Holy Spirit points out in my life or in the depths of my spirit that I didn't realize were there. Do you have that experience?

Addressing an ecumenical worship service at Harvard Memorial Chapel, Cambridge, Massachusetts, April 1982.

80
Isaiah's Experience: Confession

Isaiah's comprehension of God and his conviction of his own sin led to the third step: *confession*. Isaiah said, "I am a man of unclean lips, and I dwell in the midst of a people of unclean lips: for mine eyes have seen the King, the Lord of hosts" (Isaiah 6:5). Not only was Isaiah convicted of his sin, he confessed it openly. God will use us in the way he wants to use us if we will confess our sins and be filled with the Holy Spirit.

Are you filled with the Holy Spirit? The psalmist declared, "If I had cherished iniquity in my heart, the Lord would not have listened" (Psalms 66:18, RSV).

81
Isaiah's Experience: Cleansing

After comprehension, conviction, and confession, there was the fourth step: the *cleansing*. Isaiah said, "Then one of the seraphim flew to me, with a burning coal in his hand which he had taken from the altar with tongs. And he touched my mouth with it and said, 'Behold, this has touched your lips; and your iniquity is taken away, and your sin is forgiven'" (Isaiah 6:6-7, NASB). Notice that God provided the answer for Isaiah's sins, for coal was taken off the altar. That altar foretold the coming 800 years later of Jesus Christ, who would die on the cross. His blood would be shed and sprinkled on the doorpost of our hearts; we would be cleansed by the blood of Christ.

I don't fully comprehend that—how God could allow his Son, his only begotten Son, to be nailed to a Roman cross. And how Jesus could on that cross cry out, "My God, my God, why hast thou forsaken me?" (Matthew 27:46). For God in that mysterious moment took your sins and my sins and laid them on Christ....

Only God can forgive us and cleanse us. And he has provided that way for us as a gift to us. We don't have to work for it. All we have to do is to receive it as a gift, and he will come into our lives.

82
Isaiah's Experience: Challenge

After his cleansing by God, Isaiah accepted God's *challenge*. The challenge for all of us is to see God as he is, to see the world as God sees it, and then to step out in faith to make a difference. We read in verse 8: "I heard the voice of the Lord, saying, 'Whom shall I send, and who will go for us?'" (Isaiah 6:8)....

God wants men and women to come to know him. But they will never come to know him if they do not hear the Gospel. God looks out on this world that is in rebellion against him and alienated from him, and it breaks his heart. He is not content to stand back and allow the world to continue on its way to a Christless eternity....

God is calling us to deny ourselves and take up our cross and follow him out among the masses of people who need Christ. He is calling us to consider his call before our careers, to wrestle in prayer over the mission he has planned for us in life. God is calling us to look at the world and see it as he sees it, and answer his question: "Who will go?" What about you?

83
In the World, But Not of the World

As Christians, we are not to get our worlds mixed up.... We are not to *mingle* with the world, but we are to *witness* to the world. We are to love the world of people whom God loves. We are to weep with those who weep (Romans 12:15); suffer with those who suffer; and identify ourselves with the poor, the sick, and the needy.

Like Christ, we are to have a relationship with the world that is sociological and humanitarian, but primarily redemptive. We are to love the people of the world, not in their sins but that they might be delivered from their sins. But as for the world system of evil, we are to be separated from it.

This then is our problem: to associate with and love those who are involved in the world without being contaminated, influenced, or swayed by them. This distinction can be achieved only by a close walk with Christ, by constant prayer, and by seeking the Holy Spirit's leadership every hour of the day.

We are in the world, but the world is not to be in us.

84
86,400 Seconds, and Counting

Every morning we have 86,400 seconds before us to spend and to invest. Each day the bank named "Time" opens a new account. It allows no balances, no overdrafts. If we fail to use the day's deposits, the loss is ours.

Tomorrow will be a glorious and marvelous time for those who live in the will of God and take advantage of every moment and every second that God gives.

I speak at universities, and if I tell young people that time is short, that life is brief, they don't believe it....

Time can be our tool, but we can be its slave. Have you sat down and written out some priorities for your life? Your life ought to be carefully planned. Ask the Holy Spirit. Start going to a little place of your own where you meet God alone in prayer. Take a pencil and paper along and write out some things that God says to you.

Read Ephesians 5:16. Time is urgent; don't waste it—redeem it!

85
The Fruit of the Spirit

The moment we receive Christ as our Savior, Christ rules in our lives and the Spirit of God dominates our lives. We have the power to yield to the flesh to live a carnal life, or we have the power to yield to the Holy Spirit to live a Spirit-filled life.

If you are a Christian, which life are you living? Are you living a carnal life in which there is little Bible reading, little prayer? You go to church, but you have no daily walk with Christ, no fellowship with Christ. You do not have the joy that you know a Christian should have. Your life is an up-and-down experience.

God never meant it to be that way. God intends the Christian life to be lived on the highest possible plane at all times, bearing the fruit of the Spirit.

We cannot bear the fruit of the Spirit by our own strength. We cannot love; we cannot have joy, peace, longsuffering, gentleness, goodness, faith, meekness, and temperance by ourselves. But the Holy Spirit who has lived in us since we received Christ as Savior is the One who gives us power to love. He gives us joy. He gives us peace. He gives us patience. He bears fruit in our lives.

86
The Watermelons Told the Truth

I heard a story about a man who told his son, "Don't go into that watermelon patch. The melons aren't ripe yet." Then the father drove into town. The boy went out to the watermelon patch and found one melon that he knew was ripe. He pulled it, broke it over some rocks, and ate it. He knew he had done wrong. He knew he had disobeyed his father, but he hadn't been caught.

Several weeks passed. As the father was driving a cow up from the pasture, he saw a strange thing on the other side of the fence. He saw little watermelon sprouts by some rocks. He dug by the new plants and saw the old rinds with seeds sprouting. He knew what had happened. The boy was caught....

The Bible says, "Whatsoever a man soweth, that shall he also reap," (Galatians 6:7) and, "Be sure your sin will find you out" (Numbers 32:23).

87
Why the Statue Had No Hands

The most eloquent prayer is often prayed through hands that heal and bless. One of the highest forms of worship is unselfish Christian service. We need fewer words and more charitable works. We need less talk and more pity, less creed and more compassion....

Doctrine is important. But the Bible teaches also the importance of doing the things our Lord Jesus commands.

In the city of Strasburg, Germany, is a church that was bombed during World War II. It was totally destroyed, but a statue of Christ which stood by the altar was almost unharmed. Only the hands of the statue are missing.

The people of the church rebuilt their sanctuary, and a famous sculptor offered to make new hands to attach to the arms of the statue. But after considering the matter, the people decided to let the statue be, without hands. They said, "Christ has no hands but ours to do his work on earth. If we don't feed the hungry, give drink to the thirsty, entertain the stranger, visit the imprisoned, and clothe the naked, who will?"

Christ is depending on us to do the things that he did while he was on earth.

88
The Gospel Mended Their Marriages

Christ can transform your home…. During a Crusade meeting, a woman came to one of our workers and said, "Alcohol is making our home a hell on earth. We have little children, and my husband drinks incessantly…. We are going to get a divorce."

Then someone invited her husband to the meetings. He came forward and was converted. Theirs is a transformed home. Where once there was fear and hatred toward the father and husband, now there is love and respect for a man who has given his heart to Christ.

One evening, in another Crusade city, a well-dressed business executive came forward to accept Christ. Down another aisle came a woman who was wearing a mink coat. Both of them were converted.

As they were about to leave, they looked up and happened to catch sight of each other. Until a few months earlier they had been husband and wife. Now they were divorced. As they looked into each other's eyes, they embraced, and their tears mingled. They were remarried the next week.

"Believe on the Lord Jesus Christ, and thou shalt be saved, and thy house" (Acts 16:31). What Christ has done in other homes, he can do in yours if you will let him.

89
Pray When You're Busy

Jesus had only three years of public ministry, yet he was never too hurried to spend hours in prayer.

How quickly and carelessly, by contrast, we pray. Snatches of memorized verses hastily spoken in the morning, then we say good-bye to God for the rest of the day until we rush a few closing petitions at night. This is not the prayer program that Jesus outlined. Jesus pleaded long and repeatedly. It is recorded that he spent entire nights in fervent appeal. But how little perseverance and persistence and pleading we show!

The Scripture says, "Pray without ceasing" (1 Thessalonians 5:17). This should be the motto of every follower of Jesus Christ. Never stop praying no matter how dark and hopeless your case may seem. A woman once wrote me that she had been pleading for ten years for the conversion of her husband but that he was more hardened than ever. I advised her to continue to plead. Then some time later I heard from her again. She said that her husband was gloriously and miraculously converted. Suppose she had stopped praying after only ten years?

90
Pray Like You Really Mean It

As we observe the prayer life of Jesus, we notice the earnestness with which he prayed. The New Testament records that in Gethsemane he cried out with a loud voice, that in the intensity of his supplication he fell headlong on the damp ground of the Garden, that he pleaded until his sweat became "as it were great drops of blood" (Luke 22:44).

Too often, we use petty petitions, oratorical exercises, the words of others, rather than the cries of our inmost being. Too often, when we go to prayer, our thoughts roam. We insult God by speaking to him with our lips while our hearts are far from him. Suppose we were talking to a person of prominence, would we let our thoughts wander for one moment? No, we would be intensely interested in everything that was said. How then dare we treat the King of kings with less respect?

Pray Like You Really Believe It

J esus also teaches the victorious assurance that God answers every true petition. Skeptics may question it, deny it, or ridicule it. Yet here is Christ's own promise: "If ye abide in me, and my words abide in you, ye shall ask what ye will, and it shall be done unto you" (John 15:7). We need to trust that promise. Our Father possesses everything, and he "shall supply all [our] need according to his riches in glory by Christ Jesus" (Philippians 4:19). Let his Holy Spirit help in your prayer life just as he promised in Romans 8:27: "He maketh intercession for the saints according to the will of God" (Romans 8:27).

With God nothing is impossible. No task is too arduous, no problem is too difficult, no burden is too heavy for his love. The future with its fears and uncertainties is fully revealed to him. Turn to him, and say with Job: "He knoweth the way I take: when he hath tried me, I shall come forth as gold" (Job 23:10).

Do not put your will above God's will. Do not insist on your way. Do not dictate to God. Do not expect an immediate answer in the way, the place and the manner that you are demanding. Rather, learn the difficult lesson of praying as the sinless Son of God himself prayed: "Not my will, but thine, be done" (Luke 22:42).

92
Pray for Your Enemies

Jesus teaches us for whom we are to intercede. How startling his instructions and his example! He tells us to "pray for them which despitefully use you, and persecute you" (Matthew 5:4). In other words, he says to pray for our enemies. We are to plead for our enemies, asking God to lead them to Christ and for his sake to forgive them.

In the first words that Jesus uttered from the cross after the heavy nails had been hammered through his hands and feet, he interceded for his crucifiers, saying "Father, forgive them; for they know not what they do" (Luke 23:34). How many of us have ever spent time praying for our enemies?

We are also told in Scripture to pray for the conversion of sinners. I listened to a discussion of religious leaders on how to communicate the gospel. Not once did I hear them mention prayer. And yet I know of scores of churches that win many converts each year by prayer alone. If there is a person of our acquaintance who needs Christ in his or her life, then we need to start praying for that person. We will be amazed at how God will begin to work.

93
"To See His Face, You'll Have to Kneel."

Any day that I leave my room without a quiet time with God, I look for the devil to hit me from every angle. Power doesn't come from our own ability; it comes from God. The Holy Spirit must give a fresh, daily anointing that comes from that time you are with God. Are we men and women of prayer?…

In a city in Scandinavia is a famous statue of our Lord. A visitor, looking disappointed, was seen standing before it. He expressed to an attendant his disappointment. "I can't see the face of the Christ," he complained.

The attendant replied, "Sir, if you want to see his face, you must kneel at his feet." The visitor knelt and he saw!

We need to kneel before God, and make sure as best we know how that things are right between ourselves and the Lord—to make this moment a moment of rededication to the work to which God has called us.

94
What Do You Fear?

On the first Christmas day, the angel of the Lord told the shepherds to "Fear not" (Luke 2:10). Before Christ came, the world was filled with fear. The Romans feared rebellion, and their subjects feared Rome's power. The Sadducees feared the Pharisees, and they both were suspicious of the publicans. The hearts of people everywhere were filled with suspicion, fear, and distrust. But Jesus can put an end to fear for all who trust in him. "Fear not, little flock" (Luke 12:32) is a phrase typical of the teaching and preaching of Christ.

The world today lives with fear. Most of us fear everything except God; it is God whom we should fear most of all. However, if we are reconciled to God through Christ, we need have no fears, for "perfect love casteth out fear" (1 John 4:18)....

What is your fear? Do you fear the future with its uncertainty? Christ is the Answer to that fear. Do you fear life's burdens which sometimes seem greater than you can bear? Christ is the Answer to that fear. Do you fear death? Christ has conquered death, and if you trust in him, you can say with the Apostle Paul, "O death, where is thy sting?" (1 Corinthians 15:55). Yes, Christ is the Answer to fear.

Billy Graham preaches at the nation's capital, April 1986.

95
Thank God for His Blessings

We should be thankful for our material blessings. Some people are never satisfied with what they have. But what a difference it makes when we realize that everything we have has been given to us by God! King David prayed, "Wealth and honor come from you.... Now, our God, we give thanks, and praise your glorious name" (1 Chronicles 29:12-13, NIV).

Some years ago I visited a man who was wealthy and successful, the envy of all his friends and business associates. But as we talked, he broke down in tears, confessing that he was miserable inside. Wealth had not been able to fill the empty place in his heart.

A few hours later I visited another man who lived only a few miles away. His cottage was humble, and he had almost nothing in the way of this world's possessions. Yet his face was radiant as he told me about the work he was doing for Christ and how Christ had filled his life with meaning and purpose.

The second man was really the rich man, for he had learned to be thankful for everything God had given him. Paul declared, "I have learned the secret of being content in any and every situation, whether well fed or hungry, whether living in plenty or in want" (Philippians 4:12, NIV). A spirit of thankfulness makes all the difference.

96
Thank God for Your Friends

We should also thank God for the people in our lives. It is so easy to take other people for granted or to complain and become angry because they do not meet our every wish. But we need to give thanks for those around us—our spouses, our children, our relatives, and our friends.

Recently I received a letter from a woman who began by telling me how fortunate she was to have a kind, considerate husband. She then wrote four pages listing all his faults! How many marriages and other relationships grow cold and eventually are shattered because of fault-finding.

Do you go out of your way to let others know you appreciate them and are thankful for them? The Christians in Corinth were far from perfect, but Paul began his first Letter to them by saying, "I always thank God for you" (1 Corinthians 1:4, NIV). The Bible says that when a group of believers (whom he had never met) came out to greet Paul as he approached Rome, "at the sight of these men Paul thanked God and was encouraged" (Acts 28:15, NIV). Thank God for others who touch your life.

97
Thank God Even for Your Trials

We should thank God in the midst of trials and even persecution. We draw back from difficulties, and yet not one of us is exempt from trouble. In many parts of the world it is dangerous even to be a Christian because of persecution.

Yet in the midst of trials we can thank God because we know he has promised to be with us, and he will help us. We know that he can use times of suffering to draw us closer to himself: "Consider it pure joy, my brothers, whenever you face trials of many kinds, because you know that the testing of your faith develops perseverance" (James 1:2-3, NIV).

When Daniel learned that evil men were plotting to destroy him, "he got down on his knees and prayed, giving thanks to his God, just as he had done before" (Daniel 6:10, NIV). The Bible commands, "Be joyful always; pray continually; give thanks in all circumstances, for this is God's will for you in Christ Jesus" (1 Thessalonians 5:16-18, NIV).

I don't know what trials you may be facing right now, but God does. He loves you. Cultivate a spirit of thankfulness even in the midst of trials and heartaches.

98
Thank God for Your Salvation

We should thank God especially for salvation in Jesus Christ. The Bible tells us that we are separated from God because we have sinned. But God loves us—he loves you—and he wants us to be part of his family forever. He loves us so much that he sent his only Son into the world to die as a perfect sacrifice for our sins, and he rose again to offer us new life, eternal life. But we must reach out in faith to accept Christ as our Lord and Savior: "For God so loved the world that he gave his one and only Son, that whoever believes in him shall not perish but have eternal life" (John 3:16, NIV).

Have you opened your heart to Jesus Christ? If not, turn to him in faith with a simple prayer of repentance. If you do know Christ as your Savior, how long has it been since you thanked God for your salvation? We should not let a day go by without thanking God for his mercy and grace to us in Jesus Christ.

99
With Jesus in the Carpenter Shop

Jesus was interested in the common person. The Bible says, "The common people heard him gladly" (Mark 12:37). In fact, Jesus himself was a laboring man. In the Gospels we are told that Jesus was a carpenter. Wouldn't you like to have been able to spend a day in Joseph's little shop and watch Jesus use the carpenter's tools?

Sometimes we forget that Jesus was human as well as divine. He had calluses on his hands. If the chisel slipped and cut his finger, his blood was red and warm like ours. He knew what it meant to work long hours, to come in at night tired and weary. That is one of the reasons Jesus could say with such appeal, "Come unto me, all ye that labor and are heavy laden, and I will give you rest" (Matthew 11:28).

100
Which Is Better, Joy or Pleasure?

Are we "lovers of pleasure more than lovers of God"? (2 Timothy 3:4). Pleasures are the things that appeal to our flesh and to our lust. But joy is something else. Joy runs deep. And no matter what the climate is, what the troubles are, what the difficulties are, there is joy for the child of God, because joy is produced supernaturally by the Holy Spirit in us.

More than 40 years ago my wife and I purchased land on the side of a mountain. We built a log house out of wood from three cabins. It's a wonderful place! We have 15 or 20 springs on our property, and one spring never goes dry. We had a drought one year. All of our other springs went dry, but this one never wavered. And that's the way it is with joy. No matter what happens or how the drought comes, joy is always there, produced by the Spirit of God. Pleasure is different. It is temporary and lasts only a short season.

Jesus said, "These things have I spoken unto you, that my joy might remain in you, and that your joy might be full" (John 15:11). Do you have his joy?

101
Maintaining Your Marriage Commitment

After our commitment to Jesus Christ, our most important commitment is to our marriage vows. No matter what our feelings may be, marriage is a lifetime commitment.

Our wedding vows are a commitment made to God, to our families, to our churches, to society, in addition to each other. Commitment is the ability to stick patiently by our promises even when things are not working out as we had hoped.

Commitment means that we take constructive action. Sometimes couples need outside counsel. We need to seek counsel from those who have made a success of their own marriages. The Bible says, "Where no counsel is, the people fall: but in the multitude of counselors there is safety" (Proverbs 11:14). Seek counsel from a Christian advisor. Seek counsel from Christ. We can go straight to Jesus Christ, of whom the Prophet Isaiah wrote, "His name will be called 'Wonderful Counselor'" (Isaiah 9:6, RSV).

Get counsel from the Word of God. The Bible says, "Thy testimonies also are my delight and my counselors" (Psalms 119:24).

Make a commitment to your marriage vows, a commitment to the Word of God as your guide, a commitment to the Lord Jesus Christ as your Savior.

102
J. P. Morgan's Wealth and God's Mercy

When the multimillionaire J. P. Morgan died, his will consisted of about 10,000 words and contained 37 articles. But we are left in no doubt as to what Mr. Morgan considered to be the most important affair in his whole life. He made many transactions, some affecting large sums of money. Yet there was evidently one transaction of supreme importance in Mr. Morgan's mind. Here is what he said: "I commit my soul into the hands of my Savior, in full confidence that, having redeemed and washed it in his most precious blood, he will present it faultless before my heavenly Father; and I entreat my children to maintain and defend, at all hazard and at any cost of personal sacrifice, the blessed doctrine of the complete atonement for sin through the blood of Jesus Christ, once offered, and through that alone."*

In the matter of his soul's eternal blessing, J. P. Morgan's vast wealth was powerless. He was as dependent upon mercy as was the dying thief at Calvary. He was dependent upon the mercy of God and the shed blood of Christ just as you too are dependent.

*Frederick Lewis Allen, *The Great Pierpont Morgan* (New York: Harper Collins, 1949).

103
The Pilgrims: Firm in Their Convictions

We can learn a lot from the Pilgrims who helped found our nation. The Pilgrims left us the example of their deep, unwavering religious convictions.... They believed in Jesus Christ and his Gospel. They found fulfillment in him. They found purpose in their lives. They had encountered the living Christ, and they knew it. They feared neither the king nor any other human. They feared only God.

In our day many people are broad but shallow. Agnosticism, anxiety, and emptiness have gripped much of our world. Our youth are desperately searching for purpose and meaning in their lives. They are searching for fulfillment, which they are not finding in sex or drugs.

The Pilgrims were a group of young people, and they stand as a shining example of individuals who were narrow but deep: certain of what they believed, unswerving in their loyalty to God, and passionately dedicated to Christ whom they trusted and for whom they would have died.

I believe that a return to biblical conversion, faith, and conviction would have a great impact in our day. One of the signs I see today is that young people are beginning to look at Jesus. They are finding fulfillment in a personal encounter with him.

104
The Pilgrims: Disciplined in Their Lives

The Pilgrims also left us an example of disciplined living. The Pilgrim Fathers were Puritans who were ready to order everything—personal life, worship, the church, business affairs, political views and recreation—according to the commandments of the Bible. They lived a strict and closely regulated life. A hundred years later Jonathan Edwards wrote of the Pilgrims: "The practice of religion is not only their business at certain seasons, but the business of their lives."* They didn't mind being called "narrow" by the religious and civil establishments of the day. They remembered that their Lord had said, "Strait is the gate, and narrow is the way, which leadeth unto life, and few there be that find it" (Matthew 7:14)....

What a contrast between the conduct of the Pilgrims and the permissiveness of our day! Millions today want instant gratification. They look for all the shortcuts. There is an alarming preoccupation with self. When nations or individuals live for pleasure and the satisfaction of physical appetites, they begin to die of self-poisoning, and they most certainly will be judged severely by God.

*Jonathan Edwards, "A Treatise Concerning Religious Affections," in *The Works of Jonathan Edwards*, vol. 1, sect. 12 (London: William Ball, 1837).

105
The Pilgrims: Caring for Others

The Pilgrims left us the example of a keen social concern. They believed that every person was made in the image of God, and that each one was of infinite value and worth in the sight of God. Though the Pilgrims knew that they were citizens of another world, they sought to improve the world through which they were passing. They learned to live with the Indians who had a different religion, a different skin color and a different culture.

The Pilgrims tried to make their new world better, not by tearing down the old but by constructive toil and fair dealings with their neighbors. Today, however, we seem to think that laws and money alone can solve the great social problems and ills of our time. We have some of the finest civil rights laws in the world, but they have not solved our racial problems. Why? Because we need a change of heart and attitude. Jesus said, "You must be born again" (John 3:7). He said "I can change your life."

106
The Pilgrims: Committed to High Ideals

The Pilgrims have left us an example of commitment to great principles. The Pilgrims were idealists. They put their ideals ahead of all material considerations. It is not surprising that the Pilgrims had little and succeeded, while we have much and are in danger of failing. No civilization can make progress unless some great principle is generously mixed into the mortar of its foundations in life.

In contrast to the Pilgrims, many people today are filled with doubt. The human mind cannot remain in a state of flux. It is dangerous to let a vacuum develop. When belief goes out, doubt and cynicism may rush in, followed by tyranny, repression, and dictatorship.

A terrifying spiritual and moral tide of evil has already loosed us from our spiritual moorings. Monstrous new ideas that could easily destroy our freedoms are rushing into the vacuum.

107
The Pilgrims: Proclaiming Their Faith

The Pilgrim Fathers were evangelists who set us an example by sharing their spiritual and material blessings with others. They had agreed to "the advancement of the Christian faith," as recorded in the Mayflower Compact. The Pilgrims at Plymouth were followed by another group of Puritans at Massachusetts Bay, and both groups built churches and schools. These settlers came not simply to found a new colony but also to share their faith with the native peoples. The Puritans saw the need for continual revival and evangelism; they taught their children to be everlastingly at the task of evangelism and to maintain their spiritual lives at a red-hot glow.

Characteristic of Pilgrim preaching and of every significant Christian movement in history has been an emphasis on the judgment of God. I believe that one of the reasons for crime, perversion, and the evils of modern mankind is that we have lost belief in the certainty of God being just, holy, and righteous, and that he will judge the world.

108
The Pilgrims: Guided by Vision and Hope

The Pilgrim Fathers had vision and hope. "Where there is no vision, the people perish," says the Bible (Proverbs 29:18). The Pilgrims dreamed great dreams. They dreamed of a haven for themselves and their children. They dreamed of religious freedom. They dreamed of peace, and a stable government, churches, and schools. They dreamed of a world where God would rule in people's hearts. They lived and died with these hopes.

The Pilgrims had vision and hope because they lived in the dimension of eternity. Their strength of spirit was forged by a personal faith in God, by tough discipline, and by regular habits of devotion.

We cannot inherit these traits. But I am convinced that if we would take the traits that characterized the Pilgrims and make them our own, we could regain hope. We could recover the spiritual and moral strength that we have lost. We could offer a thrilling challenge to our young people.

109
The Ten Commandments Lead Us to Christ

Why did God give the Ten Commandments if he knew we were going to break them? He gave them in order to show us that we are sinful and weak. I look in the "mirror" of the Ten Commandments, and I say, "I am a sinner." Then I say, "God, be merciful to me a sinner!" (Luke 18:13, RSV).

God never changes. The moral law is absolute forever. God will judge us by it. His laws are irrevocable. The Ten Commandments are God's will, and we have broken them. We have sinned against his will. I see my soul before God, and I am a breaker of these laws. And that is what sin means: "Sin is the transgression of the law" (1 John 3:4).

Because I have broken God's law, I deserve judgment. I deserve hell. But God took the initiative and sent his Son to die on the cross for me and for you. God laid on him all of our broken laws. He took them for me and for you. We don't have to suffer judgment or hell. We can have "the peace of God, which passes all understanding" (Philippians 4:7, RSV). We can have the fulfillment and the joy that he produces when we give our lives to him.

How wonderful to know that all our sins can be forgiven!

At age 66, Billy Graham had preached to more people face to face than any other person in history.

110
Can Holiness Bring Happiness?

In this complex generation, it is not easy for the Christian to distinguish between that which is spiritual and that which is worldly, because Satan is "transformed into an angel of light" (2 Corinthians 11:14). He is a great imitator, and it is not always easy for us to distinguish between Satan's world and the realm where God reigns.

The happiest people I know are separated followers of Jesus Christ. They are not dependent on artificial stimulants. They do not resort to sick, dirty jokes. They do not abuse their bodies to relax their minds. The Bible says, "In thy presence is fulness of joy" (Psalms 16:11).

To be a Christian is not a pious pose. It is not a long list of restrictions. Christianity flings open the windows to the real joy of living. The world would have us believe that following Christ is nothing but "thou shalt nots." The world would have us believe that Christianity is a stolid kind of life, unnatural and abnormal.

But the scriptural evidence is to the contrary. Christ said, "I am come that they might have life, and that they might have it more abundantly" (John 10:10). Those who have been truly converted to Jesus Christ know the meaning of abundant living.

111
Are You Leading Your Family?

Christian husbands and wives are the simplest form of the local church. The Lord said, "Where two or three are gathered together in my name, there am I in the midst of them" (Matthew 18:20). Where two are gathered, just you and your wife, God is in your midst. It is a wonderful thing for children to see their father leading devotions. "Train up a child in the way he ought to go: and when he is old, he will not depart from it" (Proverbs 22:6). If anyone thinks he can train up a child in the way he ought to go and not walk that way himself, he will be disillusioned. Fathers must set the example in prayer, in Bible reading, in churchgoing, in honesty, in integrity. Children will learn far more by watching than by just listening.

Young men who are thinking about marrying should ask themselves these questions about the woman they are dating: "Can I be all this to her? Am I willing to give her myself and not just things? Am I willing to cover her faults in love with God's help? Am I willing to be patient, to cherish her as God would have me to do?" If not, then don't marry her. And the same is true for young women.

112

Are You Loving Your Spouse?

The first element in a Christian marriage—in a happy Christian home—is that the principle of love must be practiced. The Bible says, "Isaac... took Rebekah, and she became his wife; and he loved her" (Genesis 24:67). Do you love your husband? Do you love your wife? Do you tell each other that? You ought to tell each other many times a day.

Psychologists have found that touch means so much. Just touching, hugging, holding hands. How long has it been since you walked down the street holding hands with your wife? You say, "My goodness, she's gray-headed; she's old, and I'm old." I knew a couple in their nineties who walked down the street every day holding hands. What a wonderful sight it was!

"So ought men to love their wives as their own bodies" (Ephesians 5:28). "Husbands, love your wives, and be not bitter against them" (Colossians 3:19). We are to love and care for them.

113
Are You Guiding Your Children?

What about your children? The word "discipline" means to instruct. Too often the job of teaching is left to the schoolteacher, or the social worker, or the youth club leader. Whether or not we like it, life is filled with certain rules. If a child is to survive, he or she must know the rules of safety. If he is to be healthy, he must know the rules of health. If he is to drive a car, he must know the rules of the road. If he is to become a ball player, he must learn the rules of the game.

And, contrary to popular thinking, children appreciate rules. Children respect discipline. They want to be guided. It gives them a sense of belonging, a sense of security. By discipline I don't mean constant scolding or nagging or physical violence. Children do need the guidance of their parents, and we guide them more by the example we set than by any other way. We need to be firm and sane and fair and consistent—and, above all, we need to discipline in a spirit of love.

114
The Truth About Judgment

Jesus told the truth about judgment. He warned people to flee the wrath to come. If you believe a warning and act on it, it can save your life.

One evening a tornado was sighted in Colorado. The tornado warning siren sounded. The tornado struck 10 minutes later, but no one was killed. Why? Because, in large part, the people believed the warning.

Now I am warning you from the Bible, from the Word of God, that judgment is coming to you personally, to your family, to our country, to the world. God has always warned about judgment, yet we will not believe the warning. Scripture teaches us that there will be a "day when God shall judge the secrets of men by Jesus Christ" (Romans 2:16).

On Judgment Day, you will see your sins revealed to the whole world, and you will have to face them personally. We see tapes played in courtrooms to prove that people are guilty of things they deny. God too has a recording. He is not only recording all your acts; he is recording your thoughts, your intents. Jesus said, "Every idle word that men shall speak, they shall give account thereof in the day of judgment" (Matthew 12:36).

115
Hope for Changed People

The Bible tells us there can be hope for the future. First, there is the hope of a changed person. If we ever have a nuclear war, it will be because a person pushes the nuclear button or because a person overlooks something in the design of an accident safeguard. The problem, therefore, is the human race itself.

James in the Bible asked, "From whence come wars and fightings among you? Come they not hence, even of your lusts that war in your members?" (James 4:1). No matter how hard we try, we seem incapable of ridding ourselves of the selfishness and greed within us which bring conflict and strife and war. Our only hope is a changed heart.

We were created originally for God, to walk in perfect harmony with him. But we have turned our backs on God. We have chosen to go our own way. In our pride we think our way is better than God's way, and we have been paying the price of our folly. Our greatest need is to be forgiven and cleansed of sin and reconciled to God. What we need is a new heart, and that is what God offers us in Jesus Christ. God is able to change us from the inside out! This is possible because of what Jesus Christ has done for us by his death on the cross and by his resurrection.

116
Hope for a Changed World

Second, there is hope of a changed world. When we know Christ, we have a new love and a concern for others, a love and a concern which he alone can give. When we come to Christ, we can no longer be indifferent to the sufferings of others, and in Christ's name we want to do something about them. When our hearts have been changed by Christ, we can begin to help change our world. But we also have hope of a changed world because Christ has promised to come again.

No one knows exactly when Christ will come again; but we have his promise that when he comes, he will bring a new order of righteousness and peace to our world. As we read in Titus 2:13, we are to be "looking for that blessed hope, and the glorious appearing of the great God and our Savior Jesus Christ."

It seems that the word "peace" is being used more now than at any other time in history. Peace conferences are held almost daily by governments, civic organizations, and churches. But the Scripture teaches that peace and safety will not come in any lasting way until the Prince of Peace, the Messiah, Jesus Christ, comes and rules and reigns in our world.

117
Hope for an Unchanging Eternity

Finally, there is hope for an unchanging eternity in heaven. The Bible tells us this world is not all there is. Some day every one of us will die and go into eternity, whether to heaven or hell. Jesus Christ came to purchase our eternal salvation through his blood shed on the cross. We can never save ourselves or earn our right to heaven; we're not good enough. Christ did for us what we could never do for ourselves. He made it possible for us to be forgiven and cleansed of our sin, and he opened the door to heaven for us. Through faith and trust in him we can have hope—the hope of eternity in heaven.

In this world we have pain and heartache, but some day all that will come to an end for those who know Christ. The Bible gives us the glorious promise: "And God shall wipe away all tears from their eyes; and there shall be no more death, neither sorrow, nor crying, neither shall there by any more pain: for the former things are passed away" (Revelation 21:4). Yes, we can have hope—hope of a glorious eternity because of what Christ has done for us.

118
The World Will End, But We Don't Have To

The Bible says that "it is appointed unto men once to die" (Hebrews 9:27). All of nature is in the process of dying. Yet most people are living as if they think that they will never die. Most people are living for today with barely a thought of eternity.

Nature teaches, and the Bible instructs, that everything which has a beginning has an ending. The day begins with a sunrise; but the sun sets, the shadows gather, and that calendar day is crossed out, never to appear again. We will never be able to repeat today. It is gone forever.

Nations and civilizations rise, flourish for a time, and then decay. Eventually each comes to an end. This, because of sin, is the decree of history and the way of life on this planet. This is what prompted Henry F. Lyte to write, "Change and decay in all around I see; O Thou, who changest not, abide with me."

119
Peace Will Come, and God Will Bring It!

Many people are asking, "Why is there so little peace in a world of unprecedented knowledge and unlimited potential?"

We are trying to build a peaceful world, but there is no peace within people's hearts. We cannot build a new world on the old, unregenerate hearts of people. The new world will come about only when Jesus Christ, King of kings, Lord of lords, reigns supreme. He is the "Prince of Peace" (Isaiah 9:6).

The sigh of insecurity and the shouts of revolution heard across the world are perhaps the death rattle of an era in civilization, perhaps civilization as we have known it. It is God's turn to act, and Scripture promises that he will act dramatically. He will send his Son, Jesus Christ, back to this earth. He is the Lord of history. Nothing is taking God by surprise. Events are moving rapidly toward some sort of climax, but it will be according to God's time when his Son, Jesus Christ, returns to be rightful Ruler of the world.

But before that time comes, God wants to rule in our hearts.

120
Two Roads and a Choice

Some people resist the idea of a choice of any sort. They don't want to be called "narrow." But Jesus taught that there are two roads, and you have to choose which road you will take. There are two masters, and you have to choose which master you are going to serve. There are two destinies: heaven or hell. You have to make a choice.

God doesn't make the choice for us. God gave his Son who offers to forgive our sin and give us eternal life, and he helps us to make the choice by sending his Holy Spirit to convict us. But ultimately we make our own choice. God gave us the gift of free will. We can say, "I will," or, "I won't." Which will it be for you? That's the decision we have to make. We cannot travel both roads. Jesus does not allow us to be neutral about him. Jesus demands that we decide about him.

In 1993 Billy Graham's crusade in Germany was broadcast via satellite to fifty European countries.

Sources

Frontispiece, February 1992, p. 3

1. September 1986, p. 3
2. February 1993, p. 3
3. July-August 1991, p. 3
4. February 1994, p. 3
5. October 1989, p. 2
6. January 1989, p. 3
7. December 1990, p. 2
8. July-August 1986, p. 1-2
9. July-August 1986, p. 2; December 1988, p. 2
10. July-August 1986, p. 2-3
11. July-August 1986, p. 3
12. December 1990, p. 3
13. December 1985, p. 3
14. February 1992, p. 3
15. March 1993, p. 2

16. March 1993, p. 2-3
17. July-August 1985, p. 2
18. July-August 1985, p. 2-3
19. December 1992, p. 2
20. December 1992, p. 2
21. December 1992, p. 2
22. December 1992, p. 2-3
23. December 1992, p. 3
24. December 1987, p. 2
25. April 1990, p. 2
26. February 1993, p. 1
27. February 1993, p. 2
28. February 1993, p. 3
29. October 1988, p. 2
30. October 1988, p. 3
31. March 1990, p. 3
32. July-August 1994, p. 1-2
33. May 1985, p. 3
34. April 1990, p. 3
35. March 1987, p. 2-3
36. March 1987, p. 3
37. March 1987, p. 3
38. December 1990, p. 3
39. January 1985, p. 2
40. November 1991, p. 2
41. December 1985, p. 2
42. December 1986, p. 1-2
43. December 1990, p. 1-2
44. February 1992, p. 1-2

45. June 1988, p. 3
46. January 1992, p. 2
47. January 1992, p. 3
48. January 1992, p. 3
49. September 1991, p. 2
50. September 1991, p. 3
51. September 1991, p. 3
52. September 1991, p. 3
53. March 1991, p. 2
54. March 1991, p. 2-3
55. March 1991, p. 3
56. March 1994, p. 3
57. April 1988, p. 2
58. April 1988, p. 2
59. April 1988, p. 3
60. April 1988, p. 3
61. April 1988, p. 3
62. April 1988, p. 1
63. October 1989, p. 2
64. January 1993, p. 2
65. February 1991, p. 3
66. January 1989, p. 3
67. March 1985, p. 2
68. March 1985, p. 2; October 1994, p. 3
69. March 1985, p. 2-3
70. March 1985, p. 3
71. May 1993, p. 2
72. May 1993, p. 2
73. December 1986, p. 3

74. July-August 1993, p. 3
75. March 1988, p. 3
76. June 1991, p. 3
77. January 1989, p. 2-3
78. September 1988, p. 1-2
79. September 1988, p. 2
80. September 1988, p. 2-3
81. September 1988, p. 3
82. September 1988, p. 3
83. October 1991, p. 3
84. January 1985, p. 1, 3
85. October 1994, p. 1-2
86. May 1986, p. 2
87. October 1993, p. 2
88. February 1991, p. 3
89. May 1989, p. 2-3
90. May 1989, p. 3
91. May 1989, p. 3
92. May 1989, p. 3
93. July-August 1989, p. 2-3
94. December 1990, p. 2
95. November 1987, p. 2
96. November 1987, p. 2-3
97. November 1987, p. 3
98. November 1987, p. 3
99. March 1991, p. 1-2
100. October 1992, p. 3
101. June 1995, p. 2
102. April 1993, p. 13

103. November 1989, p. 1-2
104. November 1989, p. 2
105. November 1989, p. 2-3
106. November 1989, p. 3
107. November 1989, p. 3
108. November 1989, p. 3
109. April 1989, p. 3
110. October 1991, p. 2
111. May 1988, p. 2
112. May 1988, p. 3
113. May 1988, p. 3
114. July-August 1991, p. 2-3
115. January 1987, p. 2
116. January 1987, p. 3
117. January 1987, p. 3
118. September 1987, p. 2
119. September 1987, p. 3
120. September 1986, p. 3